Something for Nothing

Something for Noth

Something for Nothing

A Novel

Michael W. Klein

The MIT Press
Cambridge, Massachusetts
London, England

For information about special quantity discounts, please email special_sales@mitpress. mit.edu.

This book was set in Adobe Garamond by the MIT Press. Printed and bound in the United States of America.

Library of Congress Cataloging-in-Publication Data

Klein, Michael W., 1958–
Something for nothing : a novel / Michael W. Klein.
    p. cm.
ISBN 978-0-262-01575-2 (hardcover : alk. paper) 1. Economics—Humor. I. Title.
HB171.K54 2011
330.02'07—dc22

2010049656

10   9   8   7   6   5   4   3   2   1

For SJC

Prologue

It was all a lie.

But was that such a bad thing?

Of course, he didn't want anyone to know that he was lying. Could they tell? Did his voice give him away? His posture? His hands?

He imagined his lie made material: a bright yellow balloon floating above his head for all to see.

But if lies were material, how many balloons would there be in this room? Standing at the lectern, he looked out across the rows and rows of seats.

There would be a pink balloon floating above his best friend who was sitting in the fifth row. Did that man chatting with his friend know that the balloon was there? Had no one noticed it during the past six years?

The beautiful young woman in the third row, whose lithe body was accentuated by the way she turned to laugh at a joke from one of the people sitting behind her, had a red balloon over her head, one that he had helped inflate.

PROLOGUE

The man in the last row, the one surrounded by his acolytes, probably had twisted balloons the size of floats in a Thanksgiving Day parade hovering over him.

And that bastard in the first row, with his head inclined to the left as he shared a confidence with the person sitting next to him, he was sure there would be a whole bouquet of shiny black balloons over him, if he only could see them. He wished he could.

Yes, if lies were balloons, this room would be filled with gold and pink and white and red and black balloons. It would look like the hall at a political convention.

Balloons everywhere. There was even one big one right over this building. This building, in its own way, was a lie.

But was that such a bad thing?

He took a breath and began to speak.

"It's a pleasure to be here today . . ."

Another lie.

Labor Day

Chapter 1

"It's so hard to know what's true. You'd think that this building, with its fieldstones and ivy, was clearly meant to be part of a college. But people in town always said that old Francis Kester hedged his bets and made sure that, if his college failed, Central Hall could be just another textile mill."

David Fox, on the campus of Kester College for the first time, followed Jeff White out of the late summer sunlight and into the cool, dark entryway of Central Hall. As an untenured assistant professor in the Economics Department, Jeff's responsibilities included teaching, research, and providing new visiting professors with a tour of the campus.

It took a minute for David's eyes to adjust to the dim light in the main corridor.

"This hall does seem wide," he said.

"Yeah, but that doesn't really tell you much about original intent. So I didn't believe the story until a few years ago when there was a major renovation." Jeff laughed as he pointed to the ceiling. "A structural engineer told me that those beams were way too big for an office building, but just about the right size for a factory."

David smiled as he shifted his briefcase from one hand to the other. He found Jeff's lack of pretense refreshing. Professors in Cambridge might reveal the quirks of John Harvard, or those in New Haven might expound on the foibles of Elihu Yale, but those at less august institutions tended to be far more defensive about their colleges' reputations and, by extension, their own.

"What a great example of the specific factors model. Do you tell students about this when you teach?"

Jeff frowned. "I wouldn't do that, especially since I don't have tenure. Suppose I told my students that the founder of their college didn't really have a lot of faith in its survival, or that their parents are paying a small fortune for them to take classes in a converted factory. Things like that could come back to haunt you."

"I guess you're right." David didn't mention that he, too, would have been just as happy to remain ignorant of the fact that his first academic job was teaching in a converted factory.

But at least he was teaching. There was a period during the previous spring when it seemed that he might never find himself in front of a college class. This was especially crushing because David had begun his job search with such high hopes. Even if he wasn't the star of his graduate class at Columbia, wasn't a soon-to-be-minted Ivy League PhD a guaranteed pass to an academic career? But, as winter turned to spring, and the offers failed to materialize, he became increasingly worried that he might never realize his dream of becoming a professor. This fear peaked in late March when he received a call at his apartment late one afternoon and learned his final tenure-track job opportunity had melted away like the last patches of dirty snow on the sidewalk outside.

David tried to take this news stoically, but found himself stretched out on his couch for the next six hours. After watching the shadows creep up the wall, and then laying in the dark for much of the evening, he finally summoned the strength to get up. He crossed the small living room to the desk where he had spent countless hours over the past six years reading journals, working on problem sets, and writing multiple drafts of his dissertation. Sitting down and switching on the light, David tried to use the tools he had honed in graduate school to make sense of the whole dispiriting job search process. He took out a pad and, after staring into the airshaft for a long time, wrote the equation

Disappointment = Expectations - Outcomes

A simple equation, but one that got at the essence of his current situation.

Some solace came a few weeks later when, after a phone interview, he was offered the appointment at Kester College. He tried to avoid feeling that this one-year visiting position was a consolation prize. But that wasn't easy. After all, David's expectations had been built up for a long time. Why shouldn't the winner of the Kingsborough Elementary School math prize in third grade (the framed certificate still graced the walls of his parents' house), the recipient of an honorable mention in a Massachusetts science fair in high school (he kept that certificate in his desk drawer), and someone who graduated from Tufts University magna cum laude with honors in economics expect ongoing academic success? True, after the warm glow of college success, graduate school was like getting hit with ice water—it turns out that there are a lot of smart people out there and, for the first time, he found himself continually finishing in the middle of the pack. And it was also true that his advisor had only grudgingly approved his dissertation. But it was still a shock that this temporary job was all he had to show for six years of grinding through graduate school. When he entered Columbia, he would have been pretty disappointed if he had been told the outcome of all his hard work would be a position at Kester

College in the small town of Knittersville, New York. He would have been devastated if he also learned that this outcome was only a one-year visiting position.

David spent most of the summer coming to terms with his situation, or at least trying to. At least he had an academic job, unlike those PhDs whose hard-won expertise went unnoticed as they waited tables, drove cabs, or stood behind bookstore cash registers. And at least he had finished his dissertation; the highest degree gained by many of the other students with whom he began the doctoral economics program was the less vaunted MA or the seemingly hybrid MPhil. And at least he wasn't stuck with big student loans. "At least," however, only goes so far toward convincing you that your life's on track, especially when your point of departure is Knittersville Station.

David delayed his move to Knittersville until the end of August. This was more a result of inertia than of a continuing attraction to the Upper West Side of Manhattan, or of a desire to spend one last summer with his friends from graduate school. In fact, his relationships with his classmates at Columbia had withered over the past six months. Envy colored his relationships with his friends who, unlike him, got tenure-track appointments. Pity, and a feeling of awkwardness, altered friendships with those who were less successful than himself and had been left stranded without even a one-year visiting appointment. As a consequence, his last summer in a Columbia-owned apartment was spent mostly on his own.

After a lonely summer, and coming to a town where he knew no one, David was a little relieved that he and Jeff seemed to hit it off on his first morning at Kester College. Jeff was a couple of inches taller than David, a few years older, and showing signs of oncoming middle age, with a hairline beginning to head north and crow's feet starting to point east and west. He was obviously very bright, and had a nice sense of humor. He was also welcoming in a way that made it easy for David to get over his initial pang of jealousy when he learned that Jeff was up for tenure this coming year. If he got tenure, he would have a guaranteed job for life. Of course, if he didn't, he was out on his ass. Up or out. Publish or perish. Live or die.

But at least for this year, the careers of both David and Jeff were still alive. As these two professors of economics strode through Central Hall, the sound of their shoes against the newly shined floors echoed through the empty main corridor. Tomorrow, all would change. Students would arrive on campus. This corridor would be bustling. The bulletin boards, now mostly empty, would soon be festooned with brightly colored papers offering opportunities to join, buy, sell, travel, study, or protest.

Reaching the end of the hall, David and Jeff came to an office with an engraved copper nameplate on the door that read *Professor Geoffrey Wellingham, PhD, Chairman.* Jeff knocked lightly and a deep voice said, "Yes, please come in."

Jeff stood aside to let David in and said, "Professor Wellingham, this is our new visitor David Fox. I've been showing him the campus."

Professor Wellingham, an older man with thick white hair, round cheeks, and a ruddy complexion, rose from behind his desk and said, "Very good, White, cheers." Turning to David, he said, "Good to have you aboard Fox, nice to meet you in person. Welcome to the Kester Economics Department." After a firm handshake, the chairman gestured to an overstuffed leather chair across from his desk.

David sank back into the offered seat, his knees higher than his hips. His eyes were drawn to a large framed photograph of a gothic college building on the wall behind Wellingham. Glancing down, he noted that the chairman's desk was remarkably free of papers, books, and journals, the flotsam that typically clutters professors' workplaces. Wellingham picked up the only paper on his desk and glanced at it.

"Columbia, eh? Did you take any classes with Burlington there?" Wellingham asked with a slight smile.

"Sorry, sir, I didn't know him."

Wellingham sounded mildly reproachful as he said, "A pity that you missed meeting one of the profession's leading lights."

"Actually, sir, I believe that Dr. Burlington may have, well, I mean that actually he died two or three years before I arrived in the Economics Department."

Wellingham's eyes widened, but only momentarily. "Oh, well, no matter," he said. "I'm sure you would have learned a great deal from his advanced seminar. When he was alive, I mean." He coughed quietly and looked down intently at David's syllabus.

David, uncomfortable with the lengthening silence, finally asked, "Is that a photo of a British college?"

This question seemed to please Wellingham. "Yes, Cambridge."

"Did you get your degree there?"

"No, but I went for a term during graduate school. It was a wonderful experience. These days, Mrs. Wellingham and I try to get to the other side of the pond as often as we can. Have you been, to England I mean?"

"Only once, on a short vacation."

"Well, you must get over there; after all, it is the birthplace of our science. Smith, Hume, Ricardo, Keynes and all."

"Yes, sir, that would be nice."

"Nothing like travel to expand one's horizons. But of course, first you have some obligations here," Wellingham said with a chuckle. "So you'll be teaching a section of Principles this fall and also our course The Economics of Social Issues. Did you do much teaching while you were a graduate student?"

David's answer to this question was so well rehearsed, and repeated so often to hiring committees, senior professors, and academic deans during the previous winter, that the words came out without much effort, or much thought.

"I had some wonderful opportunities to serve as a teaching assistant, and I really valued my experience in the classroom. I've thought a lot about the way I would structure my courses, and I'm excited about the prospect of introducing students to the powerful tools that economics teaches us. I'm also looking forward to teaching more advanced students, those who are interested in delving deeper into their economics education."

Wellingham seemed pleased by this answer and unaware that he had heard it before, almost verbatim, during David's phone interview in April. "I think you'll feel right at home here, Fox. We're a small department, but we get on well with each other. The students are good, maybe not at the level of those you had at Columbia, but bright enough. And even though you are a visitor, I hope you'll feel a part of the department."

"Thank you, Professor Wellingham, I'm very pleased to be here."

Wellingham rose and came around his desk. "I'll introduce you to the department secretary, Ms. Peggy Albert, and she'll show you your office."

With some effort, David rose from his chair and followed Wellingham down the hall. He had spoken with Peggy on the phone a few times, and she seemed pleasant and efficient. As they entered her office, he was surprised to find her older than he had imagined. Her pantsuit outfit would be considered a little frumpy if not for the bright purple silk scarf draped around her shoulders.

She turned from the keyboard on which she was typing and smiled as they entered her office.

"Ms. Albert, this is our new professor, David Fox. You have his keys, I trust." Then he said to David, "Professor Fox, I leave you in Ms. Albert's expert care."

Peggy rose and extended her hand as she said, "Welcome to Kester College, Professor Fox."

David had not heard himself called "Professor" even once before, and here he had been called "Professor Fox" twice within ten seconds. He knew it was silly, but somehow, hearing those two words in a voice other than his own, made the title seem more real.

He followed Peggy up a flight of stairs and down a long corridor on the second floor of Central Hall. She turned the key in the lock of a door at the end of the corridor and stood aside as she opened the door. "Your office, Professor Fox."

Third time unlucky, at least in terms of the respect he was feeling with his newfound appellation. His swelling pride in his title was completely deflated by the sight of his new office. He knew not to expect anything like the overstuffed leather chair and the large wooden desk he had seen in Wellingham's office, but, nonetheless, he did expect better than the gunmetal gray desk, cheap chair, sagging bookshelves, broken Venetian blind, and cramped dimensions that he saw in front of him.

Peggy noticed how his face had fallen. "You know, Professor Fox, we have a catalogue that you can use to order supplies. And I even have a rug that Professor Wilson left behind after he retired that will fit right in here. That will help brighten this up. And that pile of books, Professor Van Ronan, who had this office last year, has promised to come pick them up in the next day or two."

"Thanks, Peggy. And by the way, maybe you should just call me David."

Chapter 2

"So they've got you in this shithole now."

David, who had been intently focused on the screen of his laptop, looked up with a start. He had not noticed the heavy-set man taking up most of the doorway of his office. The man, about David's own age, wearing an open-necked, striped oxford shirt and tweed coat, fixed David with a look that made it seem as if he had been watching him for some time.

"Can I help you?"

"Just here to retrieve my books."

"Oh, you must be Professor Van Ronan."

"I used to be Professor Van Ronan, now I'm just Bill."

This statement would have been more awkward had Bill Van Ronan not offered a crooked smile as he extended his hand

David rose and shook Van Ronan's hand. "It's not so bad. I spent the morning straightening it up."

"Oh, I didn't mean this office. I meant Kester."

Again, Van Ronan's smile seemed to be at odds with his words. David didn't know how to respond, so he didn't.

"I don't know why I even bothered to drive all the way from Albany to get these books. It's not like I'm going to be using them or anything. Just sentimental, I guess."

"How long were you teaching here?"

"Three years. I could've stayed around for another year, but you know, I got sick of this place. They expect you to spend 50 percent of your time on teaching, 50 percent of your time on research, and 50 percent of your time tending to students, and it just doesn't add up."

"Sorry."

"You shouldn't be. You got this job because I told them last April that I wasn't coming back. I think they were pretty desperate to find someone. Lucky for you, I guess."

David understood that this could be taken as an insult, but decided not to do so. Still, he didn't mind asking, "So where are you teaching now?"

"I'm not. I'm done with the whole academic bullshit. It's not worth it. I might go to law school, who knows."

"Are you living in Albany now?"

"Yeah, temporarily. I'm working at Capital Letters, a pretty well-known independent bookstore. You should drop by sometime."

"Thanks, maybe I will," he said with what he hoped sounded like sincerity.

Van Ronan sat down, looking like he was prepared to settle in for a nice long chat. David sat down as well and tried to signal how busy he was by putting his hands on the keyboard of the laptop.

"What've they got you teaching?"

"Principles of Economics and The Economics of Social Issues." Gesturing toward the screen of his laptop, he added, "I need to finish up the syllabi, classes start tomorrow."

Van Ronan showed no sign of taking the hint. "I taught Principles. Want some advice? Don't spend too much time preparing classes. You're just teaching straight out of the textbook anyway. And even if you do a good job of teaching, no one cares. And don't spend too much time with students; it'll do you no good."

"Thanks, I'll remember that."

"And another thing, get on the good side of the tenured faculty. It really comes down to whether they like you or not. I didn't spend enough time sucking up to them, so no one supported my case for renewal."

"That's tough."

"Yeah, well, maybe it's for the best. I thought I wanted to be a professor, but the pay's not great, you can get stuck in a town like Knittersville, and, frankly, I got bored with economics. It's better that this happened now than when I was forty, then I'd really be fucked over."

He was trying to figure out how to reply when Jeff White knocked on the open door.

"Bill, hi. How are you? What are you doing here?"

"White, how's it going? I just came to pick up some stuff I left behind. You get turned down for tenure yet?"

"Not yet," Jeff managed to say with a wan smile. "What are you doing these days?"

"I'm thinking about applying to law school, but for now I'm working at Capital Letters."

"I hear that's a great bookstore."

"Yeah, it's the last independent one in Albany. The big chain bookstores are soulless. I was telling Fox that you guys should come by sometime."

"That'd be great. David, I was going to ask if you wanted to get coffee. Bill, want to join us?"

"Nah, I've got to get back to Albany." Van Ronan scooped up his books from the floor and tucked them under his arm. "See you around, Fox. Good luck."

"Thanks. You, too. Take care."

"See you ,White. Good luck and all. Hope they don't fuck you over."

"Thanks Bill."

Jeff sat in the chair that Van Ronan had just left. After a few moments of silence, he said, "Poor bastard."

"Or just bastard?" David offered.

"Maybe, but he didn't start out that way. Bill's not dumb; he saw what was going on, how his career was going down the tubes after his first year."

"So it wasn't just that the senior faculty were out to get him?"

"No, I thought they were pretty supportive, at least at first. But his teaching evaluations started out bad and never really improved. And he pretty much gave up on research after he got a couple of harsh rejection letters from journals. I always got the impression that he liked the idea of being a professor a lot more than the work you do if you are one."

David glanced around. He had spent the better part of the morning straightening his office. Now that he had the title, even if only for a year, was he more interested in appearing to be a professor than in actually doing the work?

"I hope I didn't get into this just because I liked the idea of being a professor. Doing a dissertation wasn't much fun. It'll be pretty tough if doing research stays that hard. And I'm a little worried about teaching."

David had not meant to be so honest, but he felt the need to finally voice the thoughts that had haunted him over the past few months and, maybe, get some reassurance. What if he wasn't really cut out to be a professor? What if this was all a big mistake. But if not this, then what? There wasn't a plan B.

"Everyone starts out with doubts," Jeff said. "All you can do is try your best and not get discouraged when things aren't going well."

Not exactly the strong supportive sentiment he was looking for. Maybe Jeff had forgotten what it was like to just start out, seeing as how he was on the verge of getting tenure.

"It seems to have worked out for you."

"I could very well not get tenure."

David sensed real concern rather than false modesty. "Have you gotten any signals from the department?"

"Not really. And if I don't get tenure, then what?"

"There's always law school," David said, trying to lighten the mood with a veiled reference to Van Ronan.

Jeff seemed more wounded at this weak effort at a joke than he had at Van Ronan's pointed question about tenure. "I'm thirty-four years old, I don't want to borrow loads of money to start a whole new career from scratch."

"Yeah, I can understand that" David agreed, feeling bad about his last statement. Maybe empathy was called for here. "I really wouldn't want to be a lawyer either. I thought I might, when I was in high school, but I changed my mind the summer after my freshman year in college when I was an intern in my uncle's law office and I saw how he spent his days. I guess I don't know what I would do either, if this doesn't work out."

"I like being a professor. I like what I do in this job."

"I'm sure that you have a good shot," David said, all too aware that he had no basis for making this statement other than his first impressions that Jeff was bright and reasonable, and a good guy. He tried to continue with this line of encouragement, adding,

"Besides, even if you don't get tenure, couldn't you get a job at some other college?"

Jeff's demeanor indicated that David had missed again. "Kester's a good place, but if you get turned down here you don't have a lot of options. There are a lot of tenured professors at really good schools who didn't get tenure at Harvard, or Princeton, or Berkeley. Where do you end up if you get turned down by Kester?"

"In an independent bookstore in Albany, I guess." He was happy to hear Jeff laugh at this.

Chapter 3

David sat at a table in the kitchen of the apartment he had rented, his laptop and a cup of steaming coffee in front of him. Even on a visiting professor's salary, he could afford a decent one-bedroom apartment in Knittersville, one that was large and sunny, at least as compared to the single room in Manhattan that had served as office, bedroom, and living room when he was a graduate student at Columbia. The apartment, one of six in the building, was also only five blocks from campus, and a ten-minute walk to his office in Central Hall. This proximity was especially welcome today since it was already 9:00 and the first meeting of his Principles of Economics class would begin in a little more than an hour.

Time was pressing because of his typical close attention to detail. He was a little obsessive, sure, but his attention to detail in this case seemed warranted. After all, this was the first class offered here, or anywhere else, by Professor David Fox, PhD. Of course, obsession does not come without its traveling companion, stress. After a restless night with dreams of classrooms filled with obstructed views, chalkboards that could not be written upon, and lectures made while attired only in underwear, he got out of bed at 6:00. The cup of coffee sitting in front of him was his fourth that morning. He had also gone through more clothes changes in the past three hours than in any given three-day period when he was a graduate student. The first choice was a white shirt and striped regiment tie. Reconsidering his tie choice, he went through most all of his (admittedly meager) neckwear portfolio. He settled, or thought he had settled, on a black tie with a subtle textured pattern. But, after some inspection, it was clear that the pattern was too subtle and the black tie would cause students to think that, right after class, he would be going to a funeral. This certainly would not work in his favor, since sympathy is a cheap and ultimately ineffectual way to try to get on the good side of students. He then changed to a black shirt with the black tie to go for a monochromatic effect, a proven look, but perhaps one that had become a bit clichéd and, for that reason, desperate. Students can sense desperation in professors' efforts to be cool in the way that sharks sense blood in the water, and with much the same ultimate outcome. So, after some more consideration, a return to the original white shirt and striped regiment tie combination. Of course, this entire protracted decision-making process was the natural follow-up to his internal discussion last night that weighed the subtle messages that were conveyed by not wearing a tie (either "Hey kids, I'm not that much older than you, and I can relate to you" or "Hey, that professor's not much older than us, so he probably doesn't know what he's doing") versus those that would be sent were he to don one ("I'm the professor. You can tell because I'm dressed like a grown-up.")

After so much time spent on style, David's attention turned for one last time to substance. First lines, like first impressions, are vital. Beginning with demand and supply, the Romulus and Remus of economics, would make students' eyes glaze and make him seem like some uncool middle-aged professor (Could he somehow let on to the students that he was only 28? Should he?). He considered beginning his Principles of Economics class with the sentence "All of economics is about making choices." But, when he looked up and saw the ties littering the chair across from him, he decided to try another tack.

Why did students take courses in economics? Most did so in the mistaken belief that it was the most practical of respectable college subjects and would lead to more lucrative options than courses in philosophy, history, literature, or sociology. But it was a little distasteful to appeal to such crass motives. It was also ironic to try to sell the study of economics as a ticket to a high salary given what Kester College was paying him, someone who had devoted himself to six years of advanced study of the subject at a major Ivy League university.

David leaned back in his chair and looked at the stack of books piled across the kitchen. His eye went to the orange spine of *Freakonomics*, the book in which Steven Levitt and Stephen Dubner made economics seem cool, or at least especially clever, to a wide audience. The main lesson of *Freakonomics*, one apparent to even its most casual reader, is that people respond to incentives given the limited options they face. This single insight is the true core of economics. The rest is commentary.

Levitt and Dubner were giving him a set of examples to engage students at the outset and maybe launch them into economics with some interest in the subject for its own sake rather than with the misbegotten notion that it gave them a quick path to wealth. He went over, picked up the book, and began to page through it. This book had served only as entertainment when he first read it. Now, it promised to help him more than a black shirt/ black tie combination.

Dreams are dreams, and reality is reality, but, nonetheless, as David entered the classroom he was relieved to see that there were no obstructed seats. Placing his briefcase on the table in the front of the room, he tested the blackboard by scribbling a few lines on it with the white chalk from the tray. Still facing the board, he surreptitiously checked his zipper. Maybe this would go alright.

Turning to the class, he noticed that almost all of the seats were filled. He knew, from doing some research on Kester during the summer, that the kids sitting in these chairs were drawn from a population of students whose SAT scores were above average. But a lot of them didn't look that way. At some level, he understood that it was his own prejudices that made him question the intellectual capabilities and interests of suburban white boys who mimicked urban chic with boxers sticking out above low-slung baggy shorts, baseball caps pulled down low, and poor posture. He also knew that the upper-middle-class girls in his class who wore tight sequined t-shirts or who showed a lot of midriff weren't necessarily ditzy. But, even so, his initial thoughts, when facing the class, began, "When I was in college." He quickly recovered, however, and told himself, "Keep an open mind."

He walked around the table in the front of the class and leaned back against it. Taking a breath, he began: "I'm Professor David Fox, and this is Economics 101. For most of you, this is the first course you will have in economics, but hopefully not the last."

He paused for a second here, at his first attempt at classroom bonding, to allow the students time for a knowing chuckle, or at least a nod of agreement. But the pause proved unnecessary and led only to a few moments of still silence.

He forged ahead. "Economics is about doing the best you can, given your opportunities. So economics is mainly about incentives and constraints. Now almost all of life is lived in a way that responds to incentives and constraints, and economics lets us see how this works. Sometimes it works in ways that are surprising."

At this, David reached behind him, took his copy of *Freakonomics* out of his briefcase, and held it up. "How many of you have read this book?"

Despite years on the best-seller list, more media coverage than the author of any economics book had a right to expect, and entry of the title of the book into the common lexicon, at least around Hyde Park, Ann Arbor, and Cambridge, not one student raised a hand. Levitt and Dubner would not have been pleased.

A little shaken, but still undeterred, he continued. "Let's think about what economics has to say about buying a house. How many of your families have bought or sold a house in the last couple of years?"

A few students raised their hands warily, concerned that this might be some type of trap set by the new professor that could only end badly.

"Does anybody know what the real estate agent got as a commission on the sale of your house?"

Ah, here was the trap. The new professor was after numbers, percentages. Wisely, all the hands were retracted.

"Well, *they* would want you to think that real estate commissions are fixed, that there's no difference in the price or service realtors offer no matter who you are." He had planned, on the walk from his apartment to the classroom, just how he would pronounce the word *they*, with a subtle but unmistakable lengthening of the single syllable. *They* want to construct walls of confusion, *they* want to keep you in the dark, but *they* are afraid of the bright cold light that economic analysis sheds on *their* hypocrisy and double-dealing. What better way to get these students on his side, he thought, than to show what *they* want to hide.

The verbal emphasis on *they* did not go unnoticed. Or unchallenged.

"My dad is a real estate agent, and he doesn't cheat people," said a girl in the front row whose sequined t-shirt proclaimed that she was a "Sexy Baby."

"No, it's not cheating, not really. See, in this book," David said, now waving *Freakonomics* like a shield in front of him, "Steve Levitt shows that real estate agents act differently when it is their house that they're selling rather than someone else's."

"But you're saying that's cheating," replied Sexy Baby.

The girl sitting next to Sexy Baby, whose fashion choice made it clear to all that she wore a navel ring, added, "It's not cheating when I got meals for free at the restaurant where I worked as a waitress."

"No, this is different," he said, beginning to sense that the division between *us* and *them* was not shaping up the way he had planned. "You see, a real estate agent is supposed to try to get the highest price he can for each of his clients."

"The people who work for my dad don't cheat people either," replied Sexy Baby.

"No, no, that's not it at all." He could feel the sweat start to soak his carefully chosen shirt. "It's just that people respond to incentives."

"So is stealing responding to incentives?" one of the larger boys in the back of the class (Mets hat turned backward) asked in a way that seemed not so much a search for information as a probe for weakness.

"My dad does not steal!" Sexy Baby turned and stared at Backward Mets Hat.

"Wait, wait," David said, wanting to start over but knowing that you only get one chance to make a first impression. "Look, no one is accusing anyone of stealing. It's only like this—people want to do the best they can, but they don't steal—well, most people don't steal, but obviously some do because that's the best they can do, Levitt has a chapter on that, but I'm sure your father doesn't steal."

This was not getting better. He put *Freakonomics* down on the table, turned to the board. Time for the tried-and-true.

David drew a graph on the board, turned to the class, and said, "Most everything in economics can be understood in terms of demand and supply." To his great relief, he saw the students begin to write down what he was saying.

Chapter 4

After the longest seventy-five minutes of his life, or at least the longest seventy-five minutes since his dissertation defense four months earlier, the class ended and David gathered his books and notes. He was somewhat surprised, and even a bit relieved, when some of the students (including Sexy Baby, Navel Ring, and Backward Mets Hat) said "Bye" on their way out. He had been expecting "Good riddance."

Leaving the classroom building and emerging into the early autumn sunshine, David saw Jeff White approaching from the direction of Central Hall. Jeff noticed him as well and waved.

"So how was your first Kester class?"

"Not great. I tried to be innovative, but it got offtrack pretty quickly."

"Don't worry, by the third class the students won't remember. Hopefully they do remember something about economics. Actually, they're good kids and mostly fun to teach."

"It didn't seem like a lot of fun today."

"It will get better. My first semester was a little rough at times, but you learn what works and what doesn't."

"My first semester could very well be half of all the time I spend at Kester."

"It doesn't do you any good to think that way. Besides, it looks like we'll be hiring someone for a tenure-track position for next year. Maybe you'll have a good shot. Anyway, I'm going to get lunch, do you want to come along?"

David, taking note of the potential job opening, immediately thought about revising the chapter from his dissertation that he wanted to submit to a journal and about going over his notes for his afternoon class. But he also felt tired. He knew that he needed some sustenance, and eating alone had become a drag. In this case, the relative costs and benefits seemed easy to judge.

"Sure, that would be nice."

David and Jeff walked together to the dining hall.

College dining had improved a lot in the few years since David was an undergraduate. One way to justify high room and board fees was with a wide selection of entrees, fresh salads, and unlimited soda. It was also a way to win the battle for a bigger applicant pool and, therefore, a higher *U.S. News and World Report* rating when competing against all the other good-quality-pleasant-location-small-liberal-arts colleges. Standing in the cafeteria and reflecting on the food choices in front of him, and the quality of life battles colleges fought, David considered how this would be a good illustration of game theory for his class. But he quickly thought about the possible ways that conversation could go awry ("Are you telling us, Professor, that our food service isn't ranked third in the nation?") and decided there were enough other, more innocuous examples of the Prisoner's Dilemma.

Jeff greeted the older woman serving the salads. "Giovanna, how are you?"

She answered in a lilting voice that made it clear her origins were more likely from Napoli than from Knittersville. "Jeff, it's nice to be back with the kids. How was your summer?"

"Fine, thanks. Giovanna, this is David Fox, he's a new professor in the Economics Department."

"*Buongiorno*," David said, but immediately worried that this effort to seem friendly would be seen as condescending.

If Giovanna felt at all offended, there was no evidence of it in her cheerful reply of "*Buongiorno.*" She turned to Jeff and asked, "What is it you would like today?"

"I'll have the chicken Caesar, please, Giovanna."

She turned her attention to the ingredients in front of her and began to put together Jeff's order. It became clear when she took out the standard-sized plastic dish in which the salads were served that she had selected too much romaine lettuce and way too much chicken. But, somehow, she was able to stuff it all in and close the plastic cover.

"These dishes they give us, they are too small, *capisce?*"

Jeff smiled as he gratefully took the salad from her. "*Capisce.*"

Giovanna turned her attention to David. "You, handsome, what do you want."

"The chicken Caesar looks good."

After David and Jeff paid for their salads, and as they looked for a seat, Jeff said, "There are some of the other economists, let's join them."

Two seats were taken at the round table. An older man wearing a tweed coat and jeans sat next to a middle-aged man with bushy salt-and-pepper hair who was dressed in a short-sleeve shirt. In front of each of them was a chicken Caesar salad.

Jeff greeted them as they approached. "Hi, can we join you? This is David Fox; he's the new visiting professor."

"Murray Stern," said the man with the salt-and-pepper hair, extending his hand. David then turned to the other man and extended his hand as he said, "David Fox."

"Bob Minard."

Despite himself, he felt a bit of a quickening. The Minard Money Demand Function was part of every graduate student's tool kit and was a standard part of the first graduate course in macroeconomics. Everyone knew that Minard had developed this function as part of his dissertation. Even though he had done little research since then, this work was enough to get him a first job at Columbia, though it wasn't enough to get him tenure there. After a few stops along the way, Minard had settled comfortably into the only named chair in the Economics Department at Kester.

"Welcome to Kester," said Murray. "You're coming from Columbia, right?"

"Yes, that's right, I finished my PhD there in May."

"How's Standwell doing?" asked Minard. "Is he still trying to get that book published?"

Professor Standwell, who taught a standard first-year graduate course at Columbia, was reputedly still working on his magnum opus that would, in his opinion, finally put macroeconomics on a firm theoretical footing. So far, however, the profession had to make do with what was available.

"I had Professor Standwell for my first year macro course."

"Hope he wasn't your dissertation advisor," Minard said.

"No, he doesn't really advise many people for their dissertations anymore," said David. In fact, it was well known among the graduate students that the likelihood of completing a dissertation with a perfectionist like Standwell was about the same as that of winning the lottery, but with a much smaller payoff.

"How have you found Kester so far?" Murray asked.

"Well, my first class was a little rough," he began, but, seeing Murray raise his eyebrows and Minard look up from his salad, realized how this sounded and quickly added, "I think I'm getting the hang of it."

"You realize no one really cares about your teaching," growled Minard. "The coin of the realm is publications. And, of course, citations."

"That's true, Bob, but at places like Kester the classroom still matters," replied Murray. "Jeff's a great teacher, and he's getting papers published."

"Thanks," said Jeff. David noticed how Jeff sat up a little higher after receiving this generous compliment from Murray.

"I need to get some chapters from my dissertation in shape to send out to journals," said David. "I hope to be able to do that by the end of the semester."

"Your first semester is really tough," said Murray. "You have all those new teaching preps, and you want to keep up the momentum from your dissertation."

"And there's adjusting to living in a new city," Jeff added.

"I remember my first semester," said Minard. "In November, my paper was accepted by the *American Economic Review*. Samerstein was the editor of the journal then, so he took me out for drinks and we got hammered."

David didn't find this last comment very relevant to his own current situation, since this fall was promising to be much less successful, as well as less dissolute, than Minard's initial semester. He also thought about how his six years at Columbia were in a department quite different from the one where Minard worked as a junior professor. Legends of the old Columbia Economics Department were well known. Amazingly, despite the alleged carousing, those were also days when members of the department made important contributions to economics. By the time David matriculated, the drinking had diminished, but so had the scholarly reputation.

"David, you should think about getting your CV in shape even before you get published," suggested Murray. "If you have any papers you did for your graduate courses, you can cite them as working papers—that is, if you plan to fix them up and submit them to a journal."

"Actually, my first publication turned out to be a short paper I did for my econometrics class," said Jeff.

David did a quick mental review of his oeuvre, a task that didn't take too long. "Actually, I do have a paper from a class I could include on my CV. Thanks, Murray."

"What is it called?" asked Jeff.

"'A Difference in Difference Study of Teenage Abstinence Programs.' I got some data, fooled around with it, and found that a public school program in Kentucky that tried to get teenagers to delay their first sexual experience actually had some positive effects on teenage pregnancy rates, and even grades and behavioral problems."

Jeff laughed. "Maybe my good high school grades were a direct result of having avoided sex. But I never got a chance to do the controlled experiment."

Minard snorted, "You need a better title to get any attention. You should call the paper 'Something for Nothing.'"

The entire table laughed at that, and loudly enough to attract the attention of the students sitting around them. But, even as he was laughing, David thought about his immediate plan of action. Later, after lunch, he reflected on how the practical career advice he had received from Murray and Minard, limited as it was, still exceeded anything his advisor at Columbia had offered him during his entire last year there.

Subject: Abstract for my web page
Date: 9/7/2007, 10:42 PM
To: Liz Sparks <webmaster@kester.edu>
From: David Fox <david.m.fox@kester.edu>

Hi, Liz,

Could you please post the following paper on my personal web page, which is linked to the Econ. Dept. web page, and have a hyperlink to the abstract.

Thanks,
David Fox

"Something for Nothing: A Study of Teenage Abstinence Education Programs"
David M. Fox
Kester College

Abstract: This paper presents an analysis of a teenage abstinence program undertaken by the Department of Education of the State of Kentucky. We estimate the effects of this program using a difference-in-difference technique (from Grillincrest 1985). Pregnancy rates of high school girls are found to have been negatively affected by the program, a result that is in contrast to findings of other studies of abstinence programs, such as Kugerand 1997 and Links 1999. Surprisingly, schools that participated in this program were also found to have higher standardized test scores and lower rates of delinquency and other behavioral problems. An instrumental variables test suggests a lack of alternative driving mechanisms, although causality remains difficult to establish.

Chapter 5

"Are you busy?"

David looked up from the screen of his laptop and recognized the young woman standing at the open door of his office as a student in his Economics of Social Issues class. Jennifer something. Jennifer Lake or Jennifer McCratchen? One or the other. They were both blond and attractive, and, after two weeks of classes, he had not yet gotten their names straight.

"No, not at all. Come in."

He wasn't just being polite. He really wasn't busy, or, rather, he really wasn't productive. He had started a web search for new articles on the environmental impact of recycling. Somehow, this had turned into reading a series of articles on the Patriots' chance to go to the Super Bowl this year.

"You're Jennifer, right?"

"Yes, Jenny Lake." She brightened, seeing that the professor knew her name.

Right, Jenny Lake. Once she said that, he remembered that the way he had tried to keep their names straight was that Jenny Lake had green eyes, like lake water, while the other Jenny had brown eyes.

"What can I do for you?"

"Well, I really like your class, Professor Fox."

That was nice to hear. "Thanks very much."

"I'm a senior, and I wanted to write an honors thesis. Professor Stern told me that your research is on the economics of recycling, and I think that's a really cool topic. I was wondering if you would be my thesis advisor."

This was flattering, but a little less nice to hear. It sounded like a lot of work. He still had to prepare his lectures and try to get his own research going. It would probably take a lot of time to be someone's advisor. And he had just wasted a half hour reading about the Patriots.

"I'm not sure I'd be the right person for that."

David saw the disappointment in Jenny's face. It was a very pretty face.

"Why don't you sit down, so we can talk about this a little."

Jenny, encouraged, sat in the chair across from David and leaned forward as she handed him a thesis advisor form. David consciously focused his gaze on her face as he took the sheet from her. This took some effort since Jenny Lake had come to his office wearing a scoop neck white shirt that revealed quite a bit of lovely cleavage. Nobody dressed that way in graduate school.

David glanced down at the form. It had been neatly filled out, in a rounded script, with the proposed thesis topic "The Economics of Recycling in Knittersville."

"Why do you want to do a thesis?"

"I think it would be fun to do a research project."

David almost laughed. Fun? Fun was not the word he would use to describe the last three years as he tried to "do a research project." Nor had it been much fun over the summer, and into the fall, as he tried to revise chapters from his dissertation, with little to show for it so far. But he also remembered that he began his senior year in college excited about doing an honors thesis. Maybe he should give her a chance. But she should know what she's getting into.

"It's actually a lot of work to do a thesis, much harder than taking a class. Have you done any research projects before?"

"No, not really."

So she didn't really know what she was getting into. Could she even do a thesis? Was she a good student? She hadn't spoken much in class. This could end up being a huge time sink. Besides, who was he to advise a thesis? A few months ago he was an advisee; could he really be an advisor now?

But she certainly was an attractive student. If she did a thesis, she would be a frequent visitor to his office. That might be nice. David had not been this close to a pretty woman in a while. A woman who was only twenty-one and a student. Uh-oh. This line of thinking could be dangerous. No, it definitely is dangerous.

"Have you taken econometrics?"

"Yes, I took it last spring. I really enjoyed it and got an A."

David looked at her again. So she was bright, as well as motivated. David felt a little embarrassed, realizing his prejudices about pretty blondes.

"Have you thought about your topic? I see you have a title, about recycling in Knittersville, but you know you would need data for that. I doubt those data would be easy to find."

"Oh, there's data. I volunteer with KSA, the Kester Social Action group, and last winter we helped the mayor's office with a recycling initiative. A bunch of us helped do a survey of the town's liquor stores about how much beer they sold and how many bottles they take in for recycling. Then, in May, the town passed a law requiring liquor stores to accept empty beer and wine bottles.

John Pine, he's the assistant to the mayor, he told me I could use that data from our survey and the data from a follow-up survey that the town did over the summer."

David leaned back in his chair and looked at Jenny with fresh eyes. "Wow, that's some data set. You could get some really interesting results from that."

"I know. And Professor Stern told me you know everything about research on recycling, even the newest work."

David ruefully thought that he actually was more up-to-date with the Patriots' Super Bowl chances, but no matter.

"You know, you'll have to do some background reading first. There's a section on the syllabus for the Social Issues class on recycling, and maybe you could start with those articles."

"Oh, I read those already, and a couple of other articles, too. I made up a reading list for myself."

This time, David allowed himself a quick glance at her breasts as she leaned over to hand him a neatly typed two-page list of readings.

"This looks good," he said. She had actually done a pretty good job, for an undergraduate, in identifying the most important articles from the past ten years. She was clearly well organized. And an A in econometrics meant that she was smart as well. Maybe this wouldn't be such a bad thing to do.

"So will you do it? I mean, be my advisor?"

"Sure, let's see what happens." David signed the form and handed it back to Jenny.

"Oh, thanks so much. I just know this is going to be great."

"It's a lot of work."

"I know, but it should be fun."

'Fun' didn't necessarily seem like such a bad word after all. He looked down at the list of articles that Jenny had handed him and checked off three of them. "Start by reading these. Take some notes on them, and see if you can understand how they fit together. Then why don't you stop by next week and we can talk about these articles, and also about that data set from the town."

"Thanks again," she said, rising from the chair. "I won't take any more of your time now. See you next week."

"Bye," said David, watching her as she turned and left his office. She did seem bright. She also seemed motivated and pleasant. And, as she walked out of his office, he noticed how her tight jeans accentuated her very nice ass. "See you," he added.

Chapter 6

Far from Kester College, in a cubicle on the third floor of a newly constructed low concrete building in the foothills of rural Virginia, Greg Shankle read the Bible. Greg was not being derelict in his duties as an economics research assistant. He wasn't even demonstrating his strong devotion to his faith. He was simply responding to incentives. His work-study contract during this, his second year in the Salvation Academy for Value Economics (SAVE), stipulated that he could earn time-and-a-half during a fifteen-minute scripture break every two hours. This clause reflected the beliefs of the directors of SAVE in two sets of laws: those of economics and those of the Lord.

Greg was in line to be one of the first students granted a PhD from SAVE. He knew this program was not on a par with Stanford, Harvard, or Columbia, at least not yet. He was committed to it, nonetheless, because of its focus on using the rigorous tools of economics toward righteous ends. And, like all his classmates, he kept this focus in mind by wearing a blue rubber bracelet imprinted with the gold letters *WWJA?* (What Would Jesus Analyze?).

The SAVE program was the brainchild of Bob Dronin, a devoted Christian entrepreneur whose faith and good works had been amply rewarded with both spiritual confidence and material abundance. Dronin was the nation's largest publisher of books, videos, and CDs that reassured the faithful that, in the coming rapture, they alone would be swept up into the arms of a loving God. Dronin believed in his product. He was certain of its inherent and eventual truth. But he was also concerned that a lot of bad policies could be passed between now and the apocalypse. So he decided to recycle some of his vast fortune back to the faithful in the form of a graduate program in economics that would represent their interests. As a young man, Dronin was impressed by the tools of economics, if not the conclusions drawn by the faculty at the college he attended. He always believed economics could be used for righteous purposes. SAVE was his $40 million effort to demonstrate this to the world.

Part of this $40 million went toward the graduate education of Greg Shankle and his like-minded classmates. Another part went to fund the Center to Research Opportunities for a Spiritual Society (CROSS), an affiliated institute that was located on the same campus as SAVE. While the mission of SAVE was to train economists for future battles, the soldiers of CROSS would engage in public debate today.

As of this fall, Greg was one of those soldiers. He was offered this posting because he finished first in his class in the prelim exams in microeconomics and statistics given last spring. The job paid quite well (incentives again), at least as compared to what a grad student could make otherwise (opportunity costs and all), but it was mostly intellectual grunt work. Greg was charged with trolling the web to find research by economists, sociologists, and historians that would help shift the public debate toward the Will of the Lord. After several weeks, however, he concluded that few academics or policy analysts were producing research consistent with CROSS purposes. His classmates were not surprised when he complained of his disappointment and frustration. They knew all too well of the liberal bias of economists (along with all other social scientists). After all, as they had been taught, economists' focus on utility maximization was, at its heart, nothing more than an effort to advance secular hedonism.

Greg soldiered on in his efforts to find so-called mainstream economists whose research could contribute to the goals of CROSS. He had been told that someday SAVE would have trained enough economists to produce all the research CROSS would need, but, until that day came, intellectual outsourcing was necessary. Of course, CROSS was willing to provide monetary incentives to help support and advance researchers. The trick, however, was not getting authors to accept honoraria in exchange for publishing in the *CROSS Currents* working paper series (academic salaries being what they are), or even inducing authors to promote their own work (shameless self-promotion being as natural for academics as chasing cars is for dogs), but finding *any* work that would help promote the CROSS agenda.

The director of CROSS, Dr. William Crocker, explained all of this to Greg on the day before the beginning of the fall semester. Greg had been to Dr. Crocker's office before this meeting, and, as on each of the previous occasions, he was impressed by the modern leather chairs and couch, the sleek glass conference table, and the panoramic view of the rolling hills of Virginia. Photos on the walls showed Dr. Crocker with famous and important people (actually, Greg did not recognize most of the people in the photos, but he guessed they must be famous and important). Seated across from Greg, Dr. Crocker explained the difficulty (he used the word "challenge") that CROSS faced in finding useful research. He told him that, at this early stage of CROSS, it was natural to have one's ambition outpace one's accomplishments. Thus, at least at this point, CROSS could look outside its own bucolic campus for natural allies in its war on secularism. Normally the SAVE students were discouraged from searching the web, or from reading beyond the works assigned on their syllabi, but some venturing into uncharted waters was needed at this point.

"Who better than you, Greg, to undertake this since you have demonstrated both a commitment to the ideals of the program, as well an unusual skill in economics. You can be trusted to swim in the waters of wider research while avoiding the whirlpool of godless analysis that could spin around and confuse some of your classmates."

The combination of the furniture, the view, and the words of encouragement made Greg feel a bit dizzy. He eagerly agreed to undertake this research assistantship.

Dr. Crocker directed Greg to search for work demonstrating the benefits to individuals and society of the institution of marriage, carefully defined as the sacred bond between one man and one woman, and the evils of licentious living. At first, Greg was confident that he could find reams of research showing these results. He was wrong. Hours searching the web yielded only titles like "Marriage as a Tool of the Patrimonic Hegemon" (Sociology Department, University of Colorado), "The Optimal Length of a Marriage" (Department of Economics, University of Chicago), "Marriage and the Prisoners' Dilemma" (Economics Department, Colgate University), and "Gay Marriage throughout the Ages" (Department of History, Mt. Holyoke College). Even the one paper whose title had seemed promising, "Marriage as a Form of Optimal Commitment" (Economics Department, Swarthmore

College), turned out to be fraught with problems since its basic premise was that no one really liked to be married, but sometimes it pays off in the long run to be forced into unappealing and uncomfortable situations.

Having had no success with marriage, Greg decided to move on to sex. There had to be a lot of research showing the corrosive effects of sex outside the bonds of marriage, especially by young people. He typed "Teen Sex" into Google and evidently hit the jackpot, scoring over five million hits. Not one of which was helpful. Titles suggested that these photos had nothing to do with economic research. Greg quickly closed the screen, fearing someone walking by his cubicle might see what was on his computer. He then tried to be more careful by typing "Teen Sex Articles" into Google, but this still brought up a list of sites that, if viewed, would get him expelled, excommunicated, and damned. What if someone saw him and thought he had pulled these up for his own pleasure rather than as a way to put the world on the right path?

Greg was a bit shaken by these misdirections, and surprised to find himself sweating and breathing hard. His fifteen-minute scripture break came just in time. The gospel helped calm his mind and slow his heart rate.

He reconsidered his search strategy as he refocused on the task at hand. If not teen sex, then what? Well, not teen sex. Abstinence. And teaching teens the importance of abstinence. He typed in "Teenage Abstinence Education" into the search engine, a phrase he was sure would offer a safer set of pages. Sure enough, there at the top of the list, were a number of papers that discussed the results of abstinence education. Success at last.

Or not. As he clicked on the titles and pulled up the texts, he found himself getting more and more discouraged. The first words of the abstract of the first paper on the list, "What Is the Efficacy of Teenage Abstinence Education?" were "The short answer to the question posed by the title of this paper is 'None at all.'" The abstract of the next paper, "A Cost-Benefit Analysis of Teenage Abstinence Education," concluded with the sentence "Therefore, we find teenage abstinence education programs to have the lowest benefit-to-cost ratio of any type of wellness program, even lower than that of DARE." And it only got worse from there.

Greg finally found a paper with a more hopeful message on the fourth search page. He grew encouraged as he read the abstract of "Something for Nothing: A Study of Teenage Abstinence Education Programs" by David Fox (Kester College—where was that?). Professor Fox found that teenage abstinence programs lowered teenage pregnancy rates. Even more exciting, these programs had a positive effect on other social problems, most notably gun violence and poor school performance. Greg downloaded the paper and began to read.

Chapter 7

Kester College's Weissmuller Pool shows what happens when you assume too much. A full-length portrait of a portly, older gentleman dressed in a three-piece suit that was fashionable in the early 1950s dominates the entrance hall. The assumption made by most visitors to the pool was that Johnny Weissmuller, the Olympic swimmer and star of the Tarzan movies of the 1930s and 1940s, had really let himself go in his middle years. The truth, however, is that the pool was funded by a generous donation from Fredrick Weissmuller, Johnny's cousin. Fredrick was not as good a swimmer as his more famous cousin (after all, who was?), but he was more clever, far more successful as a businessman, and more philanthropic. His bequest funding the Weissmuller Pool came with only two provisos. One was that the pool building had a good steam room, since Fredrick greatly preferred being surrounded by hot steam rather than being immersed in cold water. The portrait in the entrance hall was his second stipulation. He knew it would contribute to the deflation of the popular image of his cousin who, during his life, never seemed to fail to mention to Frederick his conquests in the pool, or with women.

David Fox was one of those led astray by Frederick Weissmuller's puckish sense of humor. One of the first tasks he set himself in Knittersville was to memorize the open swim schedule (7:30–10:00 on Sunday, Monday, Tuesday, Wednesday, and Thursday evenings, and 1:00–4:00 on Saturday afternoons) and, ever since, he frequented the pool almost every day. Like generations before him, David often glanced at the portrait as he showed his ID to the bored student sitting at a card table in the entrance hall and thought to himself, "Boy, that Weissmuller really let himself go." And, if Johnny Weissmuller, winner of Olympic gold, could look like that, how much further mere mortals might fall. So, into the pool, to swim against the tide of aging.

Beyond its physical benefits, swimming also provided emotional ballast. He was preoccupied by Minard's lunchtime comments on the central role of research in tenure and promotion. Idle moments were often filled with strategizing about ways to revise dissertation chapters, making them suitable for submission to a scholarly journal. These ruminations generated more stress than success, however, and he felt as though his research was moving sideways, not forward. Going back and forth in the pool gave him some respite since, while swimming, he focused on the number of laps he'd completed that day rather than the number of pages he'd written that semester.

Even if his research wasn't where he had hoped it would be at this point, five weeks into the semester, he felt he had made progress in his classroom performance. The focus group–tested approach in the Principles of Economics textbook proved more successful than his initial efforts at pedagogic innovation. He also stuck closely to the syllabus he developed for his course The Economics of Social Issues. In that course, at least, he found the students more capable and more interested in the subject. This helped him relax a bit and even inject the occasional humorous comment into the discussion. For example, he broached the subject of the economics of drug decriminalization by asking the class "Why should marijuana be illegal while anyone over twenty-one can buy Scotch? After all, Scotch can lead to cirrhosis of the liver while the only long-term health consequence of marijuana seems to be . . ." At this point, he paused for a good five seconds, stared off into the distance, and finally continued by saying, "Oh yeah, memory loss." The class laughed appreciably. Later, however, he worried about his recklessness; what if his students relayed this story and word got around that Professor Fox was a pothead?

Jenny Lake could have reassured him that the joke he told in class was not out of line. She was the student he knew best and, with their weekly meetings about her thesis, the one he spoke with most frequently. But he couldn't ask her how the joke went over. He couldn't ask her much, in fact, except about her thesis. Otherwise, where would it stop: How are your other classes going? What do you want to do after you graduate? Are you busy Saturday night? Maybe he could have allowed the circle of discussion to widen beyond her thesis if she wasn't so good-looking. Maybe he could banter with her if he wasn't just a few years older, or if he was involved in a relationship. But she was beautiful and he was lonely, so he prudently kept the door to his office open whenever she was with him.

He recently started keeping his door open during the rest of his office hours as well, though in this case it was to signal availability rather than, as with Jenny, its opposite. This was a recent switch in policy. He had kept his office door closed during the first few weeks of the semester to suggest to students who might want to meet with him that he was very busy preparing classes and conducting research. Students responded accordingly and mostly left him alone. Two weeks ago, however, Ed Meade, a freshman in his Principles course, bravely knocked and requested a few minutes. After five minutes of explaining why demand curves slope down, David purposefully glanced at his watch. Ed noticed this, as David intended. Embarrassed and flustered, Ed apologized for taking up his time and quickly left. David got what he wanted and felt awful about it. Here was a kid, probably away from home for the first time, worried about his coursework, and he had blown him off. After that, he made it a point to keep his office door open and to be more welcoming. He also made sure to catch Ed after class one day and tell him to come by if he had any questions, though Ed just looked away and mumbled something about how he now understood things better.

David thought about Ed as he entered the locker room at the Weissmuller Pool, wondering if he, or any of his other students, might be there. Being relaxed with students in the classroom or his office was one thing, but feeling at ease when he was naked with them was another. He always felt a little uncomfortable changing into his swimsuit in the pool locker room. He really didn't want Mark Stanton (formerly known to David as Backward Mets Hat), Zach Rogowski (who, until he learned his name, David had called Two-Day Stubble), Peter (Can't Quite Get to Class on Time) Fisher, or any other of his male students appearing while he was naked. It wasn't because he resembled, in body type, the portly Frederick Weissmuller whose portrait welcomed the Kester community into the building. In fact, he was pretty fit, and a good swimmer, though no Johnny Weissmuller. Rather, he worried that his classroom authority might not survive a locker room sighting since, even if clothes don't make the man, nudity certainly doesn't help a lot.

Fortunately, the locker room was empty as he changed into his suit on this early October evening. The pool was also mostly deserted, with only one swimmer in lane 2 and another in lane 5. David put on his goggles, lowered himself gingerly into lane 4 (the pool never was quite warm enough to make entering it a fully enjoyable experience), and began to swim a comfortable, moderately paced crawl stroke.

When he began swimming he was about ten yards ahead of the woman in lane 5. After each flip turn, however, the distance between them shrunk, and, by his eighth lap, they had drawn even. As they swam next to each other during the next lap, nearly matching stroke for stroke, he noticed her red racing suit, her blue swim cap, her strong legs, and her attractive body. He also noticed that she was drawing ahead of him.

Now David was no more competitive than the average desperate young professor looking for a tenure-track job who realized he was engaged in a dog-eat-dog business where it all came down to the number of articles published in top journals, which, in turn, depended upon the whims of a small set of editors who most likely were just pushing the research of their own graduate students, as well as their buddies and other well-connected people, none of whom needed to teach Principles and Social Issues during their first semester out of graduate school. He began to swim faster.

With some effort, in fact with more effort than he was used to expending in the pool, he was able to keep up with the woman in lane 5. Her flip turns were faster, and so she began each lap slightly ahead of David. He would accelerate a bit and catch up with her toward the end of the pool, but, after the next turn, the chase started anew. Finally, thankfully, she swam to the wall and stopped. Of course, he could not stop then as well because it would have been too obvious that he was only swimming that fast to keep up with her. So he swam 4 more laps before finishing for the evening, albeit at a much slower rate now that his pacesetter was gone.

David was disappointed to see that, when he finished, Red Racing Suit had left the pool. He was also a little relieved—it could have been awkward if she was a student. But a lack of companionship over the past five weeks meant disappointment triumphed over relief.

He picked up his towel and went to the steam room, more tired than usual after a swim. As he entered the room, he noticed Red Racing Suit on the bench, leaning back against the tile wall. She had long dark hair and big brown eyes, features hid in the pool by her cap and goggles. Also, David was relieved to see that she was clearly not an undergraduate, but close to his own age.

"Nice race," she said.

He felt himself blush, although, between the recent exertion and the steam, she would not have noticed. "It wasn't really a race, was it?" he asked in what he hoped sounded like an innocent voice.

Red Racing Suit laughed. "No, I guess it was just a coincidence that, once I caught up with you, you began to swim faster and that somehow you managed to catch me by the end of each lap."

"I didn't really notice," he replied and, despite himself, let out a laugh.

Red Racing Suit extended her hand. "Angie."

"David."

"Do you work here?"

"This year I do. I'm teaching in the Economics Department. You?"

"My mom works on campus and I have a family pass to the pool."

"You're a good swimmer."

"You too," replied Angie. He felt a little embarrassed, but also pleased.

"I've been swimming a lot this fall." he explained. "I haven't seen you here before." Uh-oh, did that sound too much like a clichéd pickup line?

If it did, Angie didn't seem to notice. "I'm starting to get back into it. My work has been keeping me out of town the last few weeks. I hope to make swimming a more regular part of my routine." She stood up. "Well, any more time in here and I'm going to melt. See you around the pool, I hope."

Those last two words were the nicest thing he had heard in a very long time. He replayed them in his mind like an endless loop as he walked home in the cool October evening, as he climbed the stairs to his apartment and up until the moment he began to read the e-mail from greg.shankle@save.edu.

Subject: Your very interesting article
Date: 10/03/2007, 8:42 PM
To: David Fox <david.m.fox@kester.edu>
From: Greg Shankle <greg.shankle@save.edu>
Cc: William Crocker <william.crocker@cross.org>

Dear Professor Fox,

My name is Greg Shankle and I am a second-year graduate student in economics at the Salvation Academy for Value Economics (SAVE). I am working as a research assistant for Dr. William Crocker. Dr. Crocker is the head of the Center to Research Opportunities for a Spiritual Society (CROSS). My job for Dr. Crocker is to find articles that the Center can publish in its working paper series, *CROSS Currents*. I found your article "Something for Nothing: A Study of Teenage Abstinence Education Programs" on the Internet. It is really interesting how you find that abstinence programs reduce teenage pregnancy and gun violence and also raise grades.

The Center to Research Opportunities for a Spiritual Society pays researchers who let us publish their work in *CROSS Currents*. But you are still free to try to publish your paper elsewhere, although we haven't had too many problems before with people publishing their *CROSS Currents* working papers in academic journals. Also, as you may know, many influential magazines, like *Interest and the Nation, The Liberty Review*, and *Revelation and Regulation*, often discuss the research presented in *CROSS Currents* working papers, so this is a good way to get your work noticed by important people.

I hope you agree to have your paper appear in *CROSS Currents*. If you are interested, please respond to this e-mail by hitting "Reply All" since Dr. Crocker will then contact you with some guidelines for our working paper series.

On a personal note, I just wanted to say how inspiring it is for me, as a graduate student, to see a professor working on such an important moral topic.

Greg Shankle

Chapter 8

Is economics useful for everyday life? Scarcity is the central economic challenge. The most common scarce resource is time since absolutely nobody feels as if they have enough of it. Economic theory has something to say about this, about how to allocate scarce hours. If the long-run benefit to your career of an additional hour spent working on your research exceeds the benefit of an additional hour spent preparing for class, then, by all means, get that data set in order. If you have more fun (the common name for what economists call "utility") watching one more movie than reading one more book, go buy that ticket and a box of popcorn, too. A well-trained economist like David Fox knows about these calculations and should be able to draw on this theory to make his life better. But there's a big difference between knowing what you should do and actually doing it.

This was David's initial plan; get up at 7:00 each morning and, after a quick shower and breakfast, get to his office by 8:00. On Mondays, Wednesdays and Fridays, days when his first class met at 10:15, this would give him time to review for the classes taught that day. On Tuesdays and Thursdays, mornings would be spent working on research, spinning the straw of his dissertation into the gold of publications.

David mostly stuck to this plan on the days he taught. On these days, the possibility of imminent classroom humiliation helped David get out of his apartment and to his office to look over his notes for that day's classes. He also arose promptly at 7:00 on Tuesdays and Thursdays during most of September even though, by that time, he had become bored by his analysis of the effect of recycling programs on the consumption of bottled drinks. Minard's stark advice about publications as the only coin of the realm, and the thought of Bill Van Ronan behind the counter of an Albany bookstore, kept David from hitting the sleep button on his alarm clock at the beginning of the semester. But, as September turned to October, and as the sun began to rise later each morning, so did David.

Frustration certainly contributed to the slippage between David's plan and his actions. No matter how much he tried to massage the data, or change his approach, his analysis stubbornly refused to show any type of dramatic effect. David was pretty confident that there was, in fact, some small, marginal consequence of recycling on consumption, but these modest results would only be of interest to economic geeks, environmental fanatics, and his own mother. The disappointment with his research spilled over onto his actions. Recently, he began tossing his own beer bottles into the garbage rather than taking them outside to the recycle bin.

In David's mind, however, he still kept to his plan of undisturbed research work on Tuesday and Thursday mornings from the time of his arrival at his office until lunch. The thing was, he was getting to his office later and later as the semester progressed. This wasn't shirking research, it was responding to other responsibilities: keeping his apartment neat; staying abreast of current events by starting some days reading the *New York Times* at Caffeine Kerry's, the Kester campus coffee shop; and being a good colleague. He fulfilled this last obligation by stopping by Jeff White's office on Tuesdays and Thursdays. Jeff, busy as he was this semester in getting his tenure case prepared, still seemed pleased to see him. Jeff also stopped by David's office occasionally, inviting him to lunch or to go out for a beer after work. David and Jeff spent their time together talking about economics, trading some minor departmental gossip, or discussing their concerns about their jobs. But today, David felt he had something more unusual to share with his friend.

"You know, I got this weird e-mail last night," he said as he entered Jeff's office and leaned against the wall.

"Was it from the deposed finance minister's son in Nigeria? You know, it would be neighborly to let the rest of us in on these deals."

"No, that wasn't it."

"So was it an e-mail that would help you enhance your manliness with ancient herbal treatments?"

"No. And by the way, I could use the money from Nigeria, but I don't need the herbal enhancement," David protested, perhaps a bit too vehemently.

"Easy big fella. What was this strange message?"

"Have you ever heard of a graduate program called the Salvation Academy for Value Economics?"

"No."

"How about the Center to Research Opportunities for a Spiritual Society?"

"Oh yeah, I'm a member of that, I go to all the meetings."

"Well, then you must know that your Center seems really interested in my econometrics paper that we were talking about at lunch a few weeks ago, the one on teenage abstinence. I only wrote that paper for an applied econometrics course. But maybe it's pretty good after all. This Center wants to publish it in some working paper series. And they even said that they would pay me."

Jeff became serious. "You know, you have to be careful with this. You're just starting out. Do you really want to become known for your teenage abstinence paper?"

"I wouldn't mind getting known for anything, short of a capital offense."

"Really, be careful with this."

"Are you saying that my paper isn't any good?"

"David, I'm not saying that. I haven't even read that paper. All I'm saying is that you should find out more about that Center before you start getting tangled up with it."

"Well, I wouldn't have to get 'tangled up' with it if I was up for tenure this year."

Jeff frowned, and David regretted this comment as soon as he said it. He had seen how Jeff's tenure case was weighing on his mind and how he kept writing and rewriting his statement to the Promotion Committee. He knew this had not been an easy autumn for Jeff. But hell, it had not been an easy autumn for him, either. And this might be a real chance. Still, he had gone a little too far with that last statement. "Look, I'm sorry. I know you're under a lot of pressure. But this might be a good chance for me, especially since I'll be going on the job market this fall."

"Sure, fine. Just don't be stupid about this."

"Okay, okay. Good advice. See you later. Maybe we can have lunch today."

"I'll call you later this morning."

He closed the door behind him as he left Jeff's office. There was some truth to what Jeff said, to be sure, and he felt bad about not showing enough sensitivity to Jeff's position, but Jeff could play it safe since he was probably on the verge of tenure and a lifetime appointment. Jeff didn't really appreciate what it was like to be an academic nomad. Or someone with a chance to hit it big. Maybe that was it, maybe Jeff was a little jealous. He didn't have people sending him e-mails asking to promote, and pay for, his research. And besides, who was Jeff, or even David himself, to cast aspersions at what might very well be a legitimate research organization? It was just unfair, and even close-minded, not to investigate this opportunity.

He unlocked his office, sat down at his gray metal desk, and turned on his computer. He entered his ID (davidfox) and his password (pr0_fess_0r), and, as soon as the computer booted up, he went into his e-mail and reread the message from Greg Shankle. He was struck, yet again, by the fact that someone had actually read his "very interesting article," had liked it, and had even found it inspiring. Of course, Greg was a student (though he was a second-year graduate student, not an undergrad), but he was passing the work on to someone with more experience, the head of the Center to Research Opportunities for a Spiritual Society. Maybe he could get this paper published by CROSS.

Of course, a potential association with a place called CROSS, or an educational institution called SAVE made him a bit squeamish. He couldn't really see himself bragging to many of his friends, or any of his relatives, "Hey, I just got published in *CROSS Currents.*" This wasn't because of especially strong religious convictions, although David did take some unspoken pride in the over-representation of his ethnic group in intellectual achievements, especially in economics. He never told anyone this, but he had found out, from an Internet search, that more than one-third of the recipients of the Nobel Prize in Economics were members of the tribe. And there was some concern that the people at CROSS and SAVE might not welcome his participation in their organizations once they got to know his background a little better. There is no way that any but the most ignorant of the members of CROSS or SAVE would mistake him for their version of *mishpachah*.

He sat at his desk, staring at a pad of paper as he attempted to list the potential benefits and costs of responding to the e-mail and pursuing this opportunity. Time for some careful analysis. He thought about what he told his students in Principles of Economics: "Continue with a project as long as marginal benefit exceeds marginal cost." Okay, so how does that translate into this problem? What's the marginal benefit of an association with CROSS? What's the marginal cost? He had started writing down some of these ideas when there was a knock at the door.

"Come in."

Jenny Lake opened the office door and walked in. "Hi, is this a good time?"

David had taken to noticing what she wore to their regular weekly meetings. Yesterday she came in a pair of low-slung jeans and a black turtleneck. Today she was wearing a loose-knit sweater that, like the turtleneck, nicely complemented her body. "Sure," he said, "come on in."

"I'm sorry to bother you again, but I had a question about the two articles you told me about yesterday."

"Don't worry, it's really not a bother. Did you read them already?"

"No, that was the problem. I couldn't find them in the library."

"I think I may have copies. Let me look."

David rose and opened the top drawer of his file cabinet. Jenny stood behind him and looked over his shoulder. He kept his gaze on his folders, but he felt her close presence and smelled her fragrant, just-shampooed hair.

"Oh, I didn't mean for you to have to look for them, I know you're really busy."

Surprisingly, given his lack of attention to the task, David did locate the two articles. He turned around to face Jenny and found her standing closer than he had thought.

"Here they are." He looked directly into her eyes as he handed the articles to her.

She didn't avert her eyes. "Thanks. I'll make copies and get them right back to you. I know you probably need them for your research."

"No, you can keep them until next week. Actually, I'm working on some other stuff right now. A research center just contacted me and wants to publish some of the work I did in grad school."

"That's so cool. Congratulations! You must be really happy about that."

"Well, it's nice to have your work recognized."

"Totally! That's great."

"Thanks, anyone would be happy to get this kind of nice opportunity."

They stood silent for a few seconds, and then Jenny said, "Well, thanks again for the articles. I'll bring them back when we meet next Wednesday, if that's okay. Unless you need them earlier, I could stop by."

"No, Wednesday's okay. See you in class tomorrow."

"Bye, Professor, and congratulations again."

David returned to his desk, sat down, and turned his chair to look out his window. Jenny was really pretty. She wasn't coming on to him, was she? No, probably not. She was just a kid. But she was impressed by the interest from CROSS. And she was right; it was totally cool to have his work noticed. This kind of recognition could result in some good opportunities. Who knows where it could lead? He pushed the pad of paper aside, put his hands on the keyboard, and began to type.

Subject: RE: Your very interesting article
Date: 10/4/2007, 10:07 AM
To: Greg Shankle <Greg.shankle@save.edu>; William Crocker <william.crocker@
cross.org>
From: David Fox <david.m.fox@kester.edu>

Dear Dr. Crocker and Mr. Shankle,

Thank you very much for your e-mail about my article "Something for Nothing: A Study of Teenage Abstinence Education Programs." I have been working on a revision of this article and am pleased that you have some interest in it.

I would be happy to have the Center to Research Opportunities for a Spiritual Society publish a revised version of this article in *CROSS Currents* as long as I can retain rights to the article and attempt to publish it in a refereed journal. Insofar as I am not familiar with *CROSS Currents*, I would be interested in knowing what you are looking for in terms of the length of the article, the level of technical analysis, etc., and when the article might be published. Also, does this offer mean that you have essentially accepted the article and I can list it as a publication on my CV?

I look forward to your reply.

Sincerely,
David Fox
Visiting Assistant Professor
Economics Department
Kester College

Chapter 9

Bill Crocker found himself spending more and more time staring out the window of his corner office at the Center to Research Opportunities for a Spiritual Society as September turned into October. This had little to do with an appreciation of the changing colors of the trees in the Virginia foothills. Instead, Crocker's focus was on ways to grow CROSS from an acorn into a mighty oak. But his efforts had not taken root so far. Lord knows, this wasn't for a lack of effort. He had done his darnedest to make CROSS an important voice for godly analysis and a major player in bringing religion into debates on social policy. It just seemed that the soil of the secular world was more inhospitable to the seeds of religious truth than he had expected. And, to be honest, there weren't a lot of good saplings out there.

Three years ago, in his first months as the director of CROSS, Crocker came upon the little known work of Professor Roger Brockton. Brockton's research showed that regular attendance at religious services significantly contributed to higher income and greater happiness. Even better, the estimated effect was stronger for Christians than for Catholics, Jews, or Muslims. "The Protestant

Effect on Spirit and Capitalism" (a title suggested by Crocker, and accepted, after some discussion, by Brockton) was *CROSS Currents* working paper no. 001. Crocker promoted this initial publication of CROSS with a skill honed in his previous position as a lobbyist for the National Tobacco Institute. Under Crocker's guiding hand, Brockton's work gained some national media attention, as the subject of an article in *USA Today* (page 5). Following this, Crocker convinced several sympathetic columnists to mention Brockton's work to bolster their arguments about the likely outcome of the imminent clash of civilizations.

It soon became clear, however, that Crocker's skill as a publicist outpaced his abilities as an editor. The media attention attracted a swarm of researchers anxious to uproot Brockton's results. It turns out that this wasn't too hard to do. A number of articles pointed out a fundamental error in Brockton's analysis, one that should have been apparent to someone with a PhD in economics. "The Protestant Effect" quickly switched from a cornerstone of the debate on the role of religion to a loadstone that threatened to sink the credibility of CROSS. In fact, in some circles this paper became known as the "The Protestant Affect." It was cited as a prime example of poor-quality research by an economic hack who tried to gain publicity by tailoring his findings to the agenda of his paymaster. Crocker thought this unfair. He found Brockton to be a stubborn and self-righteous man who was unwilling to compromise and, unfortunately, also unwilling to listen to constructive criticism. Brockton's failure was not one of integrity, which Crocker could have accepted, but one of ability. Therefore, to avoid further embarrassment, Crocker politely declined subsequent offers from Brockton to publish more of his work.

Since that first debacle, it had become more and more difficult to find research for CROSS to promote. It wasn't so much that professors, having heard about the Brockton affair, were now gun-shy about getting their work promoted by CROSS—professors are happy to have their work cited and mentioned regardless of the publication. Rather, there seemed to be little out there that promoted a godly agenda when Crocker imposed a slightly higher bar for quality.

He had not foreseen this difficulty when he left his job working for the National Tobacco Institute. In that job, he had found no shortage of scientists who were willing to question the canards about the health effects of smoking, especially when this brave stance was rewarded with financial support for labs or funding for trips to Caribbean conferences. But, of course, the tobacco industry enjoyed extraordinary profits. Bob Dronin, while generous, was only one man and he was supporting SAVE as well as CROSS. Furthermore, Crocker had underestimated the incentives needed to start up the new field of the positive effects of religion since his initial projections were based on his experience in a well-established field, that which showed little effect of smoking on health.

Crocker eventually found a few research articles for *CROSS Currents* (working papers nos. 002–005). Unfortunately, these were modest pieces on the role of gambling casinos on local crime rates (positive), how the teaching of evolution affected SAT scores (negatively), whether megachurches deserved tax-exempt status (yes), and the market for the New Testament (burgeoning). But, unlike the Widow's Cruse, the well seemed to have run dry in the past nine months. Crocker was becoming increasingly concerned.

This concern was intensified at the summer meeting of the Board of CROSS when, during a break in the proceedings, Bob Dronin asked Crocker to come walk with him. Dronin was a cordial man, but he knew what he wanted and how to get it. He grasped Crocker's bicep in a friendly yet firm way as they walked along the stone path outside the CROSS building. "Bill, I know you're doing a fine job here, a fine job. But some of the members of the Board are starting to ask questions. A mention of CROSS in the Atlanta *Constitution* or the Dallas *Morning News* would do you a world of good. Or maybe you could get on TV with Bill O'Reilly, or get one of our CROSS researchers on Fox News. Of course, eventually those fine young people at SAVE will be giving us more research than we know what to do with. But until then, we need a bridge to the future. And Bill, CROSS is that bridge. Now, I don't want you to be worried, but maybe you could be a bit more watchful."

Crocker had become more watchful, but, despite what Dronin said, more worried as well. He decided that he needed more help in his efforts to find useful research. He hired a SAVE doctoral student, Greg Shankle, to help out. The faculty at SAVE had assured him that Shankle was their best student ever, but, at their first meeting in September, he wasn't especially impressed. Maybe the boy had brains, but he didn't seem to have a lot of sense. Greg struck him as a typical sheltered graduate student, naïve about the ways of the world and unsophisticated in how to get noticed. Still, Shankle knew a lot about using the Internet, and, at a graduate student wage, he came cheap.

Shankle had not come up with much so far, not even by the standards of working papers 002–005. But today, finally, Shankle had dropped off a paper that seemed to hold some promise. Crocker thought the title was cute, maybe a bit too cute to be taken seriously, but at least it could attract some attention. But he also thought that the abstract was pretty obtuse and the prose of the paper (at least the parts he read, the introduction and the conclusion), to be typical academic oatmeal; thick, hard to swallow, and not very tasty. He sure hoped that this Professor Fox would be more open to suggestions than Brockton had been. But even if the presentation was lacking, the substance was just the kind of thing that CROSS was looking for. As far as he understood, this paper showed that abstinence programs, programs that clearly reflected value-based teaching, had some pretty impressive results. And Shankle, who probably did understand all this, was effusive, if awkward, in his praise for the paper, both in the yellow sticky he attached to the paper and in the e-mail that he cc'd to Crocker.

Crocker turned to his attention from the paper to his computer monitor and was surprised to find a response from Fox. This was a good sign. He read the e-mail, noting with pleasure a guarded tone that nonetheless conveyed a willingness to battle public prejudices. This was a tone that reminded him of the very competent biologists he had worked with who, after some initial concerns, happily picked up the gauntlet to strike a blow against the prevailing myths about smoking. This was a very good sign. He glanced out the window and noticed, for the first time, how colorful the trees had become in the last week or so. Maybe today would be better than he had thought.

Subject: What we can accomplish
Date: 10/16/2007, 11:39 AM
To: David Fox <david.m.fox@kester.edu>
From: William Crocker <william.crocker@cross.org>

Dear Professor Fox,

It was a pleasure to receive your quick response to my assistant's inquiry. Like my assistant, I too was intrigued by your paper "Something for Nothing: A Study of Teenage Abstinence Education Programs."

As you probably know, CROSS Currents is a leading source for policy-oriented research. I would be pleased if you would agree to allow us to add your paper to our substantial list of publications.

Our authors have found that their interests and ours are aligned in efforts to publicize work appearing in CROSS Currents. We are proud of the work our external affairs department does in generating interest in our foundation's publications in widely read periodicals.

As a token of our appreciation, we would be pleased to offer you an honorarium of $500.

Professor Fox, thanks again for your quick response. I, and the staff of CROSS, eagerly look forward to a mutually rewarding relationship.

Yours,
Bill
William Crocker, PhD
Director
CROSS

Chapter 10

It was an especially beautiful autumn evening as David walked to the Weissmuller Pool. The last sunlight of the day streamed through the gold and yellow leaves of the trees at the edge of campus. The high, wispy clouds in the otherwise clear sky glowed red as the sun set. David realized, of course, that in a half hour the clouds would be dark and, in a few weeks the leaves would be down, but, for now, it was lovely.

Clearly anyone would have found this campus, on this day, at this time, a beautiful sight. But David's perception was also colored by the good news he had received earlier. After four months with very little positive reinforcement, he had reason to believe that he might, after all, be moving toward his goal of being a successful, published, respected (and someday tenured) professor of economics. He was going to have his research published in a working paper series, and, it seemed, it could even get mentioned in the press. It was a little funny to him that it wasn't his dissertation that was getting this attention, but a paper that he had completed in a couple of weeks during his third year of graduate school. He also was a little concerned about the way this paper, if not closely read, might be interpreted. But he was not so concerned that he questioned his decision to accept the offer from CROSS.

He found himself wondering whether any of his former Columbia classmates could claim popular interest in their research, especially so soon after completing their dissertation. And did any of them ever receive an offer of payment for the rights to publish their papers? As an economist, he had to honor the market. If someone was willing to pay, well then, there must be some value there. He also found himself trying to recall the amount of time between when Jeff started at Kester and when he had his first paper accepted for publication; was it two years or three? He didn't feel fully comfortable comparing himself favorably with Jeff—it felt like a bit of a betrayal to his friend—but a guy needed benchmarks. He had spent too much time already this fall using Van Ronan's aborted career trajectory as a gauge of the lower bound. It was time to move up a notch and to start comparing himself to someone more successful, someone who seemed poised for tenure. Jeff wouldn't mind.

As David turned toward the entrance to the pool, his mind occupied with the new boost given to his career, he held the door open for the woman behind him. He was delighted to discover it was Angie. He had not seen her since their initial encounter, but she had been in his thoughts repeatedly. He always scanned the lanes when he left the locker room and walked onto the pool deck, and had been continually disappointed that she was never there. He also typically loitered on the deck for a few minutes after his laps, ostensibly to stretch, but really to see if she would show up. It was ironic that their second meeting was the first time in almost two weeks that he had not spent the time during his walk to the pool to calculate the odds that she would be there. It was also fortunate, since he was more composed than he would have been if he had spent the past ten minutes wondering if he would see her.

"Thanks," Angie said as she walked through the door that he held for her. "David, right?"

He was thrilled that she had remembered his name. He, of course, had not only remembered her name, but had briefly considered having it serve as his first tattoo.

"That's right. And you're Angie?" He was proud of his feigned casual response.

"Yes, it's nice of you to remember. How have you been?"

"I'm good, really good," he replied, honestly. "How are you? I haven't seen you around the pool lately."

"I've been traveling for work. Unfortunately, I don't get a chance to swim when I travel, so you'll probably lap me tonight."

This was turning out even better than he could have hoped.

"Well, I've been pretty busy, with my research and all, so I haven't been here as much as I'd have liked either," he lied. "Still, I thought we decided it wasn't a race."

Angie laughed. He liked that laugh. He wanted to hear it more often. "See you in the pool," she said after they both showed their IDs and turned in different directions to the locker rooms.

He quickly changed, forgetting to first check whether any of his students were in the locker room. When he got to the pool deck, he found three lanes were vacant, 1, 4, and 5. He jumped into lane 4 and began to adjust his goggles in what, he hoped, would seem a casual manner.

Angie came out a minute later, in the same red bathing suit she wore the first time he saw her. He tried not to watch, or at least not to be obviously watching, as she walked along the deck and around the corner. He was relieved when she walked past lane 1 and thrilled when she jumped in next to him in lane 5.

"So what's it going to be?" she asked as she tucked her hair under her swim cap. "Want to start with a 500 warm-up?"

This was going to be a good evening, maybe the best one since the night after he passed his dissertation defense. "That's fine, just take it easy on me."

David and Angie began to swim, keeping pace with each other lap after lap. The combination of David's regular swim schedule and the intrusion of Angie's work on her exercise regimen made it easier for him to keep up with her than the last time they were in the pool together. In fact, as the first 500 turned into the second 500, and then the third and final one, he eased up so as to not pull in front of her.

After their third 500, which was to have completed their workout, she surprised him by saying, "You took it easy on me that last 500. How about we race a 50 to finish the night?"

He was pleased that she recognized he was not going full throttle and impressed by her competitive spirit. "Sure, what does the winner get?" he blurted out before thinking.

He was relieved to see that she was smiling as she answered. "Loser buys the beers." He was also really happy that their time together would not end in the pool. As far as he was concerned, he could lose the race by ten yards and still feel as if he'd won.

"Okay," he said, "go on three. One, two, three."

They pushed off the wall. David didn't take any breaths until he was halfway done the lane. Out of the corner of his eye he saw that Angie was keeping up with him. She stayed with him, stroke for stroke, as they came to the wall and did their flip turns. Off the wall, Angie had a slight lead as they headed down the lane for their second and final length. But his training started to pay off, and her travel schedule began to show. He pulled in front of her and reached the wall a half–body length ahead.

"I'll take a Sam Adams draft," he said as they both tried to catch their breaths.

"Don't gloat," she answered, smiling as she pulled off her goggles and cap. "Once I get back into training you'll be buying me dinners, not just a beer."

David liked that prospect a lot.

An increase in the New York State legal drinking age to twenty-one may not have affected overall college drinking, but it certainly lowered the amount of imbibing that took place at the establishment formerly known as The Kester Keg. In fact, the falloff in the number of freshman, sophomores, and juniors was so great that the only way to survive was to go upscale, replacing linoleum with wood, hamburgers with salads, and Miller with microbrews. The newly renamed Cask and Barrel was brighter, smelled better, and was only a bit less profitable than it was in its earlier incarnation.

David often justified a beer after swimming by thinking that, on net, he had still burned more calories than he had drunk. To-night he didn't need any justification for his after-swim brew. This was the first time he had been out with a woman since he moved to Knittersville, in fact, the first time he had been on a date in more than a year. Well, maybe a beer won on a bet didn't quite qualify as a date, but he was willing to be flexible with definitions.

David learned, on the walk from the pool to the Cask and Barrel, that Angelica DiSalluzzo was born and raised in Knittersville and, after college out of state, came back to live with her mother when her father died. She worked as a sales rep at KnitWare, one of the start-up software firms in the area. The job required more travel than she liked, but it paid pretty well, and translating computer nerd descriptions of what programs did to a language chief operating officers could understand was challenging and fun.

Angie and David found a booth at the Cask and Barrel, shed their coats, and slid onto the seats across from each other. Angie asked David about himself as she unwound her scarf from around her neck and leaned her head to the side to push back her long, dark hair. He was enchanted by these simple movements. And, in the presence of this enchantress, he found himself almost magically funny, engaging, and interesting, as he told her of his life in Manhattan. The events he recounted, while seeming to be a snapshot revealing a broad and active social life and a wide range of intellectual interests, pretty much represented all three reels of his extracurricular activities in his six years living in New York City.

"So after the bright lights of the big city, Knittersville must be pretty boring," Angie said as their beers were served.

"I'm so busy with class preparation, and trying to get my research on track, that I can't really take advantage of the Knittersville Symphony Orchestra, the Shakespeare Theatre of Knittersville, or the Knittersville Ballet."

"Too bad," she said, playing along. "I hear the Knittersville production of *Hamlet* got a really good review in the *Times*. Maybe you can catch their production of *All's Well That Ends Well* next season."

"It's not clear that I'll be around to enjoy the next Knittersville theater season," he said, a little more soberly. "Right now, I'm here on a one-year contract."

"Do you want an extended run?"

"I'd take a role in any available production at this point. A lot depends upon what happens over the next couple of months and what kind of progress I can make on my research."

"What's your research about?"

He usually avoided discussing his research, especially with women on dates, since he hoped to avoid appearing too much the geek. But Angie had asked, and she seemed genuinely interested. Also, he was emboldened by the possibility that he may soon become published and even (in a limited way) famous. So he went against his instincts.

"Actually, a think tank contacted me today about publishing one of my papers and even told me that they would try to get some attention for it in the press."

"Really, what is it about?"

"Basically, it's on the positive effects of abstinence education."

"Too bad," Angie replied with a smile that David didn't know quite how to interpret.

Chapter 11

"It was really cool. I was discussing school voucher programs in my Social Issues course, and this student, Jason Baugh, asked how we could know whether better school performance was because the schools were better, or because parents who decided to use the vouchers were more involved with their kids' education. That's a pretty subtle point for a sophomore to think up on his own."

David and Jeff were entering the dining hall as David excitedly recounted how Jason's point started a class discussion on methodology. David tried to raise the more general point that the conclusions drawn by an author of a study may not be the most valid reading of the evidence. He thought that this would be a difficult point to make to students used to treating whatever they were handed as definitive. Much to his surprise, however, students seemed liberated, rather than threatened, by his line of argument. Drawing on the readings from the first half of the semester, they began to apply this general idea to the specific topics covered in the course so far. After the first few minutes of this discussion, when questions were directed to him ("Professor Fox, didn't that article about Headstart say that it worked?"), students found they did not need his validation of their ideas, and they began to address each other ("Yeah, Steve, but remember that other article about teacher's unions showed there was no effect"). David literally stood back and watched what he had wrought, thinking that he now understood more clearly what it meant to teach people how to think for themselves.

Jeff nodded as David told him about the class. He then said, in a mock conspiratorial tone, "Since I'm up for tenure this year, you shouldn't breath a word of this to anyone, but I really find teaching a lot of fun."

He understood perfectly why Jeff would not want his love of teaching well known at this moment in his career. Tenure is based on teaching and research. Many promotion committees, despite their public pronouncements, consider success in one of these activities possible only at the expense of the other. Consequently, teaching is a relatively low hurdle in most tenure cases; basically, showing up to class, covering the textbook material, and avoiding personal invective are all that's required. Maybe this is because of the difficulty in measuring teaching "impact." Research impact, likewise, is somewhat vague, but at least there are a number of quantifiable indicators: the number of published books and articles; the ranking of journals in which the articles appear; the number of citations (minus the number of self-citations). It is so rare as to be almost unknown for a tenure case to fail because of excellent research but poor teaching. The ranks of nomadic visiting professors, however, are filled with those who had been judged excellent teachers but inconsequential contributors to research in their fields.

These basic truths about academic success were driven home to David throughout his graduate studies. The indifference that he often detected in his professors' classroom performance contrasted strongly with the impassioned presentation of their own research that he witnessed in seminars or at conferences. As he learned more about academia, he realized that this made perfect sense; you don't get to be a professor at Columbia because of what you teach, rather because of what you have published. But, even knowing this, he had been a little surprised that this ethos had permeated the profession beyond the top graduate departments to places like Kester. Minard's admonishment, "The coin of the realm is publications," stayed with him throughout these first eight weeks of the semester. Actually, "haunted him" might be a better term. He still wasn't making great progress with his dissertation chapters. Up until today, he had felt some resentment at the long hours he spent preparing for class. But the dividends paid in the last hour had begun to shift his view. And it also helped that some of the research pressure had been relieved by the prospect of CROSS publishing his work.

David and Jeff got into line and found Giovanna at her regular post. Jeff ordered the standard chicken Caesar salad, and Giovanna expertly stuffed the generous portion into the miserly plastic container. David, contrary to his habit over the past six weeks, paused for a minute before ordering, considering the other salad options on the board behind Giovanna. Maybe today was ripe for all sorts of new experiences.

"You're David the swimmer, right?" Giovanna asked.

He was caught off guard. He looked at Giovanna, who had what seemed like a familiar smile on her face, and replied, "Well, I do use the pool often. How did you know that, Giovanna?"

"My Angelica told me she swam with you last night."

He felt his face grow hot. "Yeah, we saw each other at the pool. I didn't know Angelica was your daughter."

"Sure she is. So you want your regular chicken Caesar?"

"That would be great Mrs. DiSalluzzo, I mean, Giovanna, thanks."

It didn't seem possible, but Giovanna packed even more food into his container than she had into Jeff's. "*Buongiorno*," she called after them brightly as they went to pay for their purchases.

"What was that all about?" Jeff asked as they settled into a table in the corner of the cafeteria.

"You know how I go swimming most evenings? Well, this woman, Angie, uses the pool as well. She's a really good swimmer. We've seen each other there a few times, and last night we went out for a beer after our swim. I had no idea she was Giovanna's daughter."

"That was pretty obvious from your reaction."

"I was worried, the first time I saw her, that she might be a student, but she's my age."

"There's no faster way to lose your job here than to get entangled with a student. It seems like a generation ago, sleeping with your students was viewed as part of the compensation package. But today, it's a sure way to get the boot, even if you have tenure."

David looked at Jeff. Was this a specific warning, or just a general statement? Had he mentioned anything to him about Jenny Lake? He thought of her standing close to him in his office, closer than he had realized. Not that he minded. But nothing had happened, and nothing was going to happen. He didn't like the way this conversation was going.

"What do you do for dating?" David asked. He had not broached this subject before, feeling that it was intrusive. But he wanted to change the path of the discussion. Besides, if Jeff could be witness to his discomfort with Giovanna, then this question seemed fair.

"David, I'm gay," Jeff said, fixing him with a look to gauge his response.

"Yeah, but what do you do for dating?" he replied. He did think to himself, however, that you can learn a lot about a person in eight weeks and still not know some central things. This thought was immediately followed by his grateful realization that, after eight weeks of growing familiarity, you can find out in an instant that you have become a trusted friend.

He could see, in the broad smile that he received from Jeff, that his nonchalant response was a relief. David had a number of gay and lesbian friends in college and graduate school. At one level, Jeff's preferences did not seem like a big deal. But he also understood that Knittersville was not Manhattan. The environment of a small college in a little town could be a breeding ground for concerns about professors' lifestyles, especially when a lifetime appointment of tenure was under consideration. Jeff was right to be careful about sharing details of his personal life.

"Well, I certainly would avoid the bars in Knittersville, if there were any," Jeff said. "There's more of an open scene in Albany, and it's not that far from here. In fact, I just started dating someone there who I like."

"So, what's his name?" David asked in his best imitation of his grandmother's inquiries to him (though her questions employed a different gender of the possessive pronoun).

"Mark, and he works in a bank. We've been seeing each other for a month or so, and we're getting along really well."

In a more serious tone than his last question, he asked, "I guess I should keep mum about this, huh?"

"Thanks for asking. Murray knows. I suspect other people in the department also know, but it's mostly 'Don't ask, don't tell.' So it might be best not to mention Mark to anyone, and, besides, I don't want you to jinx the relationship just as it's starting."

"Mind if I join you?" David and Jeff looked up, both a bit startled, since they had not noticed anyone approaching the table.

"Oh, hi, Randolph. Sure, sit down. David, this is Randolph Carlson. He teaches sociology. Randolph, this is David Fox, he's new to the Economics Department this year."

Randolph was a tall man with a slightly protruding belly. A guess placed him in his early to mid-forties, judging by his salt-and-pepper hair and the gray in his goatee. He wore blue jeans, a work shirt, loafers, and a tweed coat. He extended his hand to David as he sat down.

"So another apologist for the capitalist system of oppression," Randolph said with a smile, or perhaps it was a smirk, as he shook hands.

"No, just a guy trying to make an honest buck." Randolph immediately reminded him of some of the sociology grad students he'd met at parties in New York, a memory not recalled with particular fondness. Fueled by alcohol and self-righteousness, they often asked him whether he really believed the arcane nonsense they were teaching in the Economics Department, and whether he realized the damage that economics had done to the working people of the world. He felt put back on his heels immediately by these comments and often came up with clever retorts, but, unfortunately, these came to him the next day, long after they would have been helpful.

"Is there such a thing as an 'honest buck'?" Randolph asked, raising one eyebrow.

"There is if you teach kids the laws of economics instead of moldy old Marxist analysis," Jeff answered.

"Laws were made to be broken," Randolph said. "Especially those that oppress."

"So what do you teach?" asked David, who, despite his visceral dislike of Randolph, would have been happy to see the conversation become more amicable. David felt that this question would help toward this goal since, he knew, professors were never as happy as when discussing themselves.

"I'm teaching a seminar, Fighting Globalization, where I show the kids how to recognize and fight corporate control of the economy. Part of the requirement for the course is to get involved in a direct action to support workers in struggling countries. This semester, I'm requiring the kids to start a campus boycott of coffee that isn't shade-grown and isn't sold by cooperatives run by indigenous people. I'm also teaching a lecture course, Threats to Liberty, where I point out the conformity demanded by the right wing, and how this oppresses freedom of thought and action."

"Sounds interesting," said David in what he hoped was a convincing tone of voice.

"Oh, it's not just interesting, it's empowering."

Failing to detect any hint of irony or self-deprecation in Randolph's expression,, David decided to get his coffee to go today. Feeling a little guilty for leaving Jeff with Randolph, but not so guilty as to not do it, he begged the forgiveness of his two lunchtime companions, saying he had get ready for class.

"More graphs to prepare to illustrate empty theory?" said Randolph with what might have been a tone of derision.

"No, I have to look over some real-world data. Count yourself lucky that your courses don't require any of that." As he turned to leave, he saw Jeff smile at him.

Chapter 12

It appeared to be a butterfly.

Jenny Lake had come to David's office for her regular Wednesday meeting about her thesis. In the last two weeks, David had found himself less focused on her body, and more on her mind, since he had shifted his ongoing interest in the female physique from Jenny to Angie. But it was hard not to notice her attractive body this afternoon, on the last day of October, since she came to his office dressed in a white full-body leotard. The only way David could avoid staring at her body was to focus on the small image painted on her face, just below her right cheekbone. It appeared to be a butterfly.

"I read the two articles you told me about, but I had some problems understanding the model in the first one. What do they mean when they call something a separating equilibrium?"

"An example of a separating equilibrium is when you initially can't tell what type of person someone is, but then their actions tip you off to what they're like. For example, whether they are high-skilled or low-skilled, or whether they're trustworthy or not."

"Oh, okay, I see now."

"Jenny, I have to ask you, why do you have something painted on your cheek. Is that a butterfly?"

She laughed, a little self-consciously, but also a little coquettishly. "There's a big Halloween party tonight, and I won't have time to get ready for it later this afternoon, so I got into costume already." She held up a shapely leg so David could see her foot and said, "See my toe shoes? I'm going as the ballet of Madame Butterfly."

"Isn't Madame Butterfly more famous as an opera?"

"Yeah, but I look better in a leotard than an opera gown, don't you think?"

David felt a stirring deep in his chest. She looked really good in a leotard. But he also knew better than to answer that question. Maybe he would have answered it a couple of weeks ago, before he and Angie had started seeing each other. He had been a bit more playful with Jenny in their conversations from one week to the next, and she seemed to have become more comfortable, and more informal, during their weekly meetings. But, even then, he remained mindful of what Jeff had told him, that there was no quicker way to get himself in trouble than to come on to a student. He was sure that this was true even if it was the case that she came on to him first.

"So do you have any other questions about the articles?"

Jenny saw that her last question had made her professor a little uncomfortable, and that she might have crossed a line. "No, thanks for your time."

"You're welcome. Have fun at your party."

"Thanks. Hope you have a nice Halloween, too."

Jenny rose and walked out of his office. In the last two weeks, David had tried to stop following her exit with admiring eyes, but today, given how she was dressed, he couldn't help himself. "Trick or treat," he thought.

Watching Jenny walk away, he also thought that Angie was just as pretty as she was. Some women, like Angie, start out pretty in their early twenties and become more beautiful as they approach thirty. And he imagined that Angie, with her fine features and strong, trim body, would be considered beautiful no matter what her age. But it was way too soon to start thinking about Angie in her mid-thirties or forties, wasn't it?

Of course it was. But it had been a great two weeks, maybe the best he had since college. After that first date at the Cask and Barrel (given what happened subsequently, he thought it was appropriate to call the conversation over those first beers a date), he and Angie arranged to go out two days later to a Friday night dinner in Albany. He was nervous as he walked up the steps to the front porch of her mother's house, and he felt butterflies in his stomach as he rang the bell. Giovanna answered the door and welcomed David warmly. Angie told her mother not to wait up (which he took as a good sign) and followed him down the steps to his car.

Angie had just finished an intensive two-week period of travel and seemed to really enjoy the chance to unwind at dinner. Her stories of her recent travel showed that she had a good sense of humor and a keen ear for the absurd. He particularly enjoyed her story about the young hotshot consultant she met, born to wealth and on track to even greater riches, who said he enjoyed helping young rich Internet entrepreneurs because it provided him with a sense of, as he put it, "giving back to the community."

David's contributions to the conversation were less funny than Angie's, but heartfelt. He mentioned his initial doubts about coming to Kester but, as the semester progressed, how he was growing more fond of the college. He told her a bit, but not too much, about his new friend Jeff who was facing a tenure decision this year. He recounted the story of the students in his Social Issues class becoming increasingly savvy about economics. He discussed the challenges in teaching first-year economics to freshmen. He didn't happen to bring up anything about his work as a thesis advisor.

As they walked back to David's car after dinner, Angie took his hand. He felt his heart race. They held hands during the entire ride back to Knittersville. He considered asking her whether she would like to come up to his apartment for a drink, decided against it because it seemed too forward, but then decided it was worth a shot. Angie said, "A drink would be nice," but, once they got into the apartment, they were in each other's arms before a bottle could be opened. They kissed on the couch for a while, her body molding to his. Then, without a word, he stood up and took her by her hand into the bedroom (which he had purposefully straightened up earlier that day). He had imagined this moment since that first evening he met her at the pool. He knew her body from those times in the pool, up to what was concealed by a thin layer of lycra, but here, in his bedroom, he gained full knowledge of it.

They lay next to each other afterward, still holding hands. "That was really nice," she said.

He turned on his side, propped up on his elbow, and looked into her eyes, and asked, "Nice?"

She laughed. "Okay, great."

"Great?"

"Really superb?"

"You're getting closer."

"Well, what would you call it?"

"The best ever."

"Really?"

"Yeah, really."

She gave him a kiss. "You're sweet."

They both fell asleep for a little while, Angie on her side and David curled around her. Angie woke first and shook him awake. "Can you give me a ride home?"

"Sure," he said, and they both got dressed. It was well after midnight, and the streets of Knittersville were empty as he drove her back to her mother's house. The house was dark when they arrived.

"What are you doing tomorrow?" David asked.

"It is tomorrow," she replied.

"What are you doing today?"

"Not much. Catching up with all the stuff I missed when I was traveling, I guess."

"Want to have breakfast?"

"David, it's only a few hours until breakfast."

"Ok, how about lunch?"

"How about coffee? We could meet for coffee this afternoon."

"Great, I'll come by to pick you up."

"No, why don't we just meet in town. I'll meet you at Starbucks at 3:00."

"Okay, see you then."

They kissed once more, and David watched Angie as she walked up the steps. He figured that it was only thirteen hours until he saw her again. Somehow, he found a way to fill those hours.

Chapter 13

"They say Lark Street is Albany's Greenwich Village."

"Jeff, Albany doesn't have a Greenwich Village."

"Okay, David, you've made your point. We're not in Manhattan, but at least Jeff's trying to be positive about this trip."

"Angie, I'm not being negative, just realistic."

"Realism is a social construct."

David turned his eyes from Lark Street to look at Angie, sitting in the passenger seat across from him, and smiled despite himself. "What did you say?"

"David, everyone knows that realism is a social construct. And right now, you're not being very sociable." Angie laughed after she said this.

"And you're not being very constructive, either," Jeff offered from the backseat.

"Okay, okay. Point taken." David stopped at a red light and pointed at two old men on the sidewalk. "Hey, isn't that Allen Ginsberg walking with Bob Dylan over there?"

"That's a howler, Mr. Bohemian Manhattan," Angie said.

"That's Dr. Bohemian Manhattan to you," he corrected her.

It actually was pretty attractive here, David thought to himself. The brownstones lining the street would not have seemed out of place in New York City. On this first Saturday in November, a cool but sunny afternoon, it was lively as well. Many of the brownstones served as shops and featured brightly colored signs. Young people, families with small children in strollers, and older couples holding hands filled the sidewalks. Okay, it wasn't Manhattan, but he would have never found a parking spot in Manhattan and there was one just waiting for him up ahead.

Angie had suggested this excursion. She noticed that David was becoming more tense as the deadline for submitting applications for this year's academic job market approached. He initially told her that he couldn't take off the whole day and, besides, he had made plans to meet Jeff for coffee. She told him it would do him good to get a little distance from his work, and from Knittersville, and besides they could invite Jeff to come along. She added that it would be a nice chance to meet David's closest friend on campus. After thinking about it, David decided that he was happy to have his new girlfriend meet his favorite colleague. And, as it turned out, Jeff was happy to go along. After hearing so much about Angie from David, he wanted to see what all the fuss was about.

David parked, and the three of them got out of the car and began to stroll around, David with his arm around Angie's shoulders and she with her arm circling his waist.

"When I was in high school we used to drive here on weekends and get coffee," Angie said. "We felt so cool. There was nothing like this in Knittersville."

"Caffeine Kerry's wasn't around then?" Jeff asked.

"It was, but we didn't go on campus. It seemed off-limits."

"It's an open campus, isn't it?" David asked.

"It wasn't anything official, but it just didn't seem right," Angie explained.

"Well, how about we relive your youth and get a coffee now?" David suggested.

"Hey look," Jeff said, "it's Capital Letters, the place Van Ronan works. Let's check it out."

David wasn't as enthusiastic as Jeff about seeing the former occupant of his office, but he was willing to see what the last independent bookstore in Albany looked like.

It looked like all the other independent bookstores that David had ever been in. Bookshelves made of unpainted plywood were filled with a mixture of hardcover and paperback books of various vintages. Hand-lettered signs pointed customers in the direction of the sections covering different subjects; American history, music, Judaica, gay studies, sociology, religion and occult (a single category). Every Barnes & Noble bookstore had a section on business, but Capital Letters didn't. Then again, no Barnes & Noble bookstore had a separate section on revolution and radical history.

David instinctively started looking for the economics section. He thought he might locate a first edition of Samuelson, or an old copy of Pigou. But before he could find one of these famous economists, an ex-economist found him.

"Shit, Fox, you actually showed up. How you doing?" Van Ronan was wearing the same tweed coat as on the day he showed up at Kester. He enthusiastically shook David's hand. He then raised an eyebrow and asked in a conspiratorial tone, "They kick you out already? You looking for a job?"

"No, I'm good, Bill. Thanks anyway. We were in the neighborhood and thought we'd check out the place."

Hearing Van Ronan's voice, Jeff came over to greet him. "Hey Bill, how's it going?"

"Good, really good, White. You get the bad news about tenure yet?"

"No, I think they're waiting for my birthday to turn me down."

David knew Van Ronan was joking, maybe it was even good-natured (though it was a little hard for him to see that), and Jeff did seem to play along, but it pained him nonetheless.

Angie came over and David put his arm around her.

"So who's this?" Van Ronan asked with a smile and an appreciative look up and down her body.

"Angie, this is Bill Van Ronan. He used to work at Kester. Bill, this is Angie DiSalluzzo."

"Hi," said Angie.

"Hi," said Bill and then, turning to David, asked, "Where'd you meet her?"

"Angie's from Knittersville."

"No shit?" Van Ronan asked with real surprise in his voice.

"No shit," Angie replied, with a sudden edge in her voice. "David, I'm going to check out the feminist literature section. You boys have a nice chat."

"Whoops," said Van Ronan, though he didn't look like his faux pas concerned him much. "Sorry about that, Fox."

David was sorry about that, too. In fact, he was sorry that he had agreed to come into the bookstore at all. "Yeah, well, okay."

"So how fares old Kester? Students any smarter this year?"

"There are always some good ones," Jeff answered. He, too, looked like he was reconsidering the wisdom of visiting the bookstore.

"So Fox, where you gonna be next year? Any leads?"

This was, of course, the very question that had occupied David all morning and had made him less than a cheerful presence during the drive to Albany. He had anticipated spending most of the day working on his research so he would have a paper in good shape that he could include with his applications. The original plan for the day included a break for coffee with Jeff, but only a break for an hour or so before getting back to work. Now it looked as if the whole day would be shot. He and Angie were planning to go out for dinner this evening, but even with that he had figured that he would have been able to get in a solid six hours today. As it was, he did zilch. He wasn't really angry at Angie for having talked him into this, but he wasn't really pleased either.

"Nothing concrete yet, but I did get an offer from a think-tank to compensate me for publishing one of my papers in their working paper series."

It gave David a little pleasure to see Van Ronan a bit taken back by this. He also noticed, however, that Jeff looked a bit bemused.

"Well, good for you Fox. I wish you a lot of luck," Van Ronan said with what seemed to be sincerity.

"Thanks, Bill. Well, good to see you. We've got to be going now."

"Hey, you want to see something funny? There's this novel by an economist that just turned up. I was looking at it last night. The guy tries to be witty, but he should have stuck to his regressions."

"Maybe next time," said David. He and Jeff had already started to leave and Angie, noticing them moving toward the door, joined them. "Take care, Bill."

"You, too. Good luck, White. Nice to meet you, Angie."

"Bye," she called over her shoulder and then, in a whisper that only David and Jeff could hear, "asshole."

Once they were outside, Jeff apologized for dragging them into the bookstore. Angie told him that it wasn't his fault. David, with his hands thrust deeply into his pockets, tried to figure out whether he would have any time to work later this afternoon, after they got back to Knittersville.

As they walked down the street, searching for the coffee shop that Angie frequented in her youth, Jeff said, "Well, it could have been worse."

"How do you figure that?" David asked.

"We could have bought that novel."

Thanksgiving

Subject: Summary of Professor Fox's article
Date: 11/09/2007, 11:05 PM
To: William Crocker <william.crocker@cross.org>
From: Greg Shankle <Greg.shankle@save.edu>

Dear Dr. Crocker,

I have finished my three-page summary of Professor Fox's article, "Something for Nothing: A Study of Teenage Abstinence Education Programs," and I left a copy for you in your office. If I may say so, I think this article will be really good for CROSS. Professor Fox shows that there were some really positive benefits when the State of Kentucky introduced a program to teach teenage abstinence. As you might have guessed, teenage pregnancy rates fell. But what was really surprising is that standardized test grades improved in the schools teaching the program, and there were even effects on behavior—there were significantly fewer cases of guns being brought to school. So this really shows how values education helps a lot.

I know you are anxious for me to check out the accuracy of the results. I sent an e-mail to Professor Fox to ask for his data and programs. As soon as I get this, I will start working on it.

Again, I want to thank you very much for the opportunity to work for you, especially on such an interesting and important project.

Sincerely,
Greg Shankle

Chapter 14

Greg was looking forward to the upcoming Thanksgiving holiday, he really was. In a few days, there would be a big turkey dinner with his family. Then after dinner, just as in the past, he would join his younger brothers, his dad, and his grandpa in the rec room to watch football on TV. His mom would pamper him— the son who went away to college—during the rest of the weekend, baking his favorite Rice Krispies squares and serving these to him along with a big glass of milk.

Greg liked spending time with his family. But ever since he started graduate school, he had been worried that they thought he was getting uppity. There wasn't any one obvious tip-off. In fact, maybe he was the only one who noticed all the little things that made it seem as if he didn't fit in so well anymore. Like the way that he tuned out conversations about the goings-on in the town that he left six years ago. And the fact that he no longer played basketball in the driveway with his younger brothers (although now he was the shortest and slightest of the Shankle boys, and this might have been a factor, too). Or how it had become a family joke that he fell asleep on the couch right after Thanksgiving dinner each of the last six years. "Bored by football?" his Dad would ask him, as if the very idea were absurd. But, to tell the truth, Greg did find football boring, even though it was the combined effects of tryptophan and the long hours studying and working in the preceding weeks that sent him into a deep sleep after only a quarter or so of gridiron action.

The one part of the long Thanksgiving weekend that remained special, year after year, was the opportunity for Greg to spend time with his grandpa. Grandpa showed a real interest in Greg and in his studies. Greg wouldn't tell anyone this, but he had the sense that he was Grandpa's favorite. One time his dad more or less confirmed this, commenting on how Grandpa was so proud that someone in this generation did so well in college, and even went on to graduate school, since no one in Grandpa's day had the chance to finish high school, much less attend college.

Despite a lack of formal education, Grandpa had always read widely. Greg was impressed by this. He was also impressed by the kind of questions that Grandpa asked him about his studies and about economics in general. When Greg was an undergraduate, Grandpa asked him why people lost jobs, whether buying cars from foreign countries hurt America, and if helping rich people ended up hurting working people. Greg answered these questions to the best of his abilities, drawing on what he had been taught in college. Grandpa listened with interest and always picked up the gist of the argument quickly. Greg felt some satisfaction in thinking that he was contributing to his grandpa's education, even in a small way. These discussions also demonstrated to him the vast gulf between the chances he was given and the limited choices facing his grandpa when he was young, during the Great Depression. He liked to think that his opportunities were, even if only very indirectly, opportunities for his grandpa as well.

Last year, however, Greg found it much more difficult to share his learning with his grandpa. The material in the first year of graduate school was much more technical than what he learned in college and, frankly, a lot less focused on the real world. What could Greg tell his grandpa about bordered Hessians, the calculus of variations, or Inada conditions?

But this year he felt that he would have more to share. Greg had recently completed writing up a summary of Professor David Fox's paper for Dr. Crocker. He knew that Dr. Crocker had a PhD, and could have done this himself, but basic comparative advantage arguments taught him that there were more efficient uses of the time of the director of CROSS. This type of efficiency argument was even stronger in the case of Greg's next big project, which he had just begun: checking all the statistical work in Professor Fox's paper. Professor Fox had been very kind, and had responded quickly to his request for his data and computer programs. With these in hand, he would soon begin replicating the results. Greg suspected that Dr. Crocker could have done this on his own faster and better than a mere graduate student. But, as with the summary of the article, it made sense for him to check the analysis and for the director of CROSS to attend to his more pressing duties. Despite this natural division of labor, Dr. Crocker's obvious and often-voiced concern that Professor Fox had not made any errors made Greg proud that he was chosen to undertake this task.

Greg's positive first impressions of "Something for Nothing: A Study of Teenage Abstinence Education Programs" were partly based on his view that its findings validated choices he had made in his life. Well, technically, choices wasn't the right word since his continuing abstinence had more to do with a lack of opportunities than with actions taken, or more accurately not taken, in the heat of the moment. Still, the important point was that he had remained pure. Consistent with the results in Professor Fox's paper, this purity was associated with his academic success (and also consistent with the paper's findings he had never been involved in any acts of gun violence). Whether this was an example of causation or correlation, he could not say.

Greg could say, however, that Professor Fox's command of the literature was impressive, as was the way the paper's findings were placed in the context of existing research. His admiration grew when he discovered that Professor Fox had only recently completed his PhD. This meant he must have written the paper as a graduate student. Greg did not think he could write a paper with that level of sophistication at this point in his career. He found it even harder to imagine any of his classmates doing so. This wasn't as much a reflection on the abilities of any of the students in SAVE as it was on the program itself. The professors employed by SAVE, as well meaning as they were, did not offer the same level of training that Professor Fox must have received at Columbia. He had to admit to some disappointment when he figured this out. He was able to keep his spirits up by remembering that the V in SAVE stood for Value. He and his classmates, unlike students elsewhere, studied and learned in a way consistent with the question on the bracelets they all wore, *WWJA?*

There wasn't much left of the turkey, or of the stuffing, mashed potatoes, creamed corn, minted peas, or Jell-O mold. Greg's mom, aunt, and grandma had shooed the men out of the kitchen, though it wasn't really that hard to convince the male Shankles to go to the family room. Greg's dad and grandpa had loosened their belts and were in the matching La-Z-Boy recliners. Greg and his youngest brother, Grover, sat on the couch. The twins, Graham and Grant, lay on the floor. Everyone had their eyes fixed on the TV, watching the game.

Chicago had returned the opening kickoff to its own 35 yard line. The Detroit defense was able to stop the Bears from getting a first down. The Lions received the punt and began their first possession deep in their own territory.

"How's school going, Greg?"

"Great, Grandpa, really great. This year I'm starting to do some work for an institute at the school called the Center to Research Opportunities for a Spiritual Society. I get paid pretty good, and I do some interesting work for them."

The Lions got a first down, and then another. Their drive stalled, however, and they were forced to punt. The Chicago offense took the field again.

"What kind of interesting work?" his grandfather asked.

"Well, this institute likes to get people to see economic research that has a godly theme. My job is to find research on the Internet. I found a paper that the director of the institute, Dr. Crocker, really liked. I had to summarize the paper for him, and now I'll do some fact-checking."

The Lions were able to stop the Bears again before they could get a first down. Detroit then got the ball and, on the third down, a long pass went just beyond the hands of the wide receiver who had gained two steps on the free safety. The Lions had to punt again.

"What's that paper about?" asked Grandpa.

"This professor at a college up north shows that kids at high schools that have teenage abstinence programs don't get in trouble and even get better grades than kids at high schools that don't have these programs."

"We had to sit in on one of those programs," Grant said, "and it was really boring."

"Yeah, it sucked," Graham agreed. "And it made it a lot harder to get girls."

"That's enough of that kind of talk," their dad said.

Chicago fumbled on its second down, and Detroit took possession on the Chicago 30 yard line. Three plays later, the Lions scored the first touchdown of the game.

As the commercial started, Greg's grandfather said, "Greg, it just makes sense to teach kids values. Kids need to learn what's right and what's wrong, and schools should do that. What are you all trying to prove with this research?"

Greg would have answered something to the effect that not everyone was like them, and a lot of people questioned whether schools should teach values, so it was good to show that these programs worked. He would have also mentioned that there are lots of different values programs out there, and it is important to be able to judge which are the most effective since there are scarce educational resources. And finally, research like that of Professor Fox helped shape the agenda and put the country on a more godly path. But Greg's grandfather, whose eyes had been fixed on the television screen, didn't see that Greg couldn't answer because, just before the Detroit fullback ran 6 yards into the end zone, Greg had fallen into a deep sleep.

Greg's dad looked over and, seeing his oldest son asleep, just shook his head.

Subject: Getting your work noticed
Date: 11/22/2007, 10:23 AM
To: David Fox <david.m.fox@kester.edu>
From: William Crocker <william.crocker@cross.org>

Dear David,

I am encouraged in the way that we are moving forward together. Your research has caused quite a stir here, and all those who have had the time to read it carefully, myself included, are impressed by your work and excited about your results.

David, your role is to generate this research and our role is to get it noticed. With this in mind, I have prepared the following two press releases that CROSS will circulate. One of them is for our traditional constituency, while the other is for a more mainstream audience. You'll notice that I have shortened the title and punched up some of the results to make the paper more accessible to an audience that does not share our level of technical sophistication. Let me know if you have any suggestions, but, in the interest of time, I am going to go ahead and start to get this out there in the public forum.

I have instructed my people to cut a check for you for $500. I know that this is a little premature, since your paper has not officially appeared yet, but take it as a mark of my confidence in you and also a hope that, as they say in the movies, this is the beginning of a beautiful friendship.

Best wishes for the Thanksgiving holiday.

Yours,
Bill
William Crocker, PhD
Director
CROSS

PRESS RELEASE
FOR IMMEDIATE RELEASE

Center to Research Opportunities for a Spiritual
Society (CROSS)

Research Shows Benefits of High School Abstinence
Programs

Teenage abstinence programs are an important part of
a values education. Recent research sponsored by CROSS
(The Center to Research Opportunities for a Spiritual
Society) demonstrates that, in fact, the positive effects of these programs go well beyond what was tradi-
tionally believed. In a *CROSS Currents* working paper,
Professor David Fox (PhD Economics, Columbia University)
shows that high school teenage abstinence programs significantly reduce teenage pregnancy rates. But, surprisingly, these programs also have strong positive effects
on behavioral challenges facing high schools, and even
academic performance. As with some of the other research
published in the *CROSS Currents* working paper series,
Professor Fox's timely and seminal paper demonstrates
the importance of values-based education in our schools.

For more information, contact:
Dr. William Crocker, Ph.D., Director, The Center to
Research Opportunities for a Spiritual Society
william.crocker@cross.org

PRESS RELEASE
FOR IMMEDIATE RELEASE

Center to Research Opportunities for a Spiritual
Society (CROSS)

Abstinence Pays Off

While we learn from The Word that "the wages of sin is
death" (Rom. 6:23), research sponsored by CROSS (The
Center to Research Opportunities for a Spiritual Society) shows that the return on investment in godliness
can be well above market. Professor David Fox of Kester
College has shown, in a *CROSS Currents* working paper,
that high school teenage abstinence programs are effective well beyond what we could have prayed for. Professor
Fox demonstrates that teaching our children respect for
their bodies and themselves has the expected result of
reducing teenage pregnancy, which, of course, has implications for the ongoing genocide of fetal deaths. But,
even beyond this, these programs have a significant effect on instilling values in our children that result in
lower gun violence (thus reducing the need for government
intrusion in the free exercise of the Second Amendment)
and in better performance on standardized tests that are
needed to ensure schools leave no child behind. These
tremendous returns show how values education pays big
dividends and are well worth the investment.

For more information, contact:
Dr. William Crocker, PhD, Director, The Center to
Research Opportunities for a Spiritual Society
william.crocker@cross.org

Chapter 15

Thanksgiving was a workday for Bill Crocker and had been for some time. When employed by the National Tobacco Institute, he invited a number of his tobacco industry clients to Thanksgiving each year ("This turkey's so good because it's smoked" always got an appreciative chuckle). Now, as the director of CROSS, he and his wife Sally played host to some of the organization's trustees. There was little difference between the extent of holiday preparation back when he worked for the National Tobacco Institute and those he currently faced as the director of CROSS. Nor was there much difference in the level of pre-holiday stress. The only real difference, as far as Crocker was concerned, was that his daughter Tricia was no longer in attendance. After an argument during which Tricia yelled "Thanksgiving is not 'Take your daughter to work day,'" the family negotiated a deal. Tricia would come home for Christmas (and have the opportunity to collect her presents at that time), and, in exchange, she did not have to play the role of the dutiful daughter on the fourth Thursday in November, a part for which she had no natural talent.

Tricia's mother did not have the same choice available to her. Sally Crocker knew it was her duty to be a gracious hostess, initially for gatherings of clients of the National Tobacco Institute and, during the past three years, for the trustees of the Center to Research Opportunities for a Spiritual Society. Sally was nothing if not practical. She understood that her spa treatments, vacation house, clothing allowance, and Lexus depended upon her successfully playing a particular role, especially on days like Thanksgiving. But, like an actress in a long-running, lucrative, but somewhat trite play, she lacked the enthusiasm she had when she created the role. Nonetheless, as with any successful thespian whose livelihood depends upon her craft, Sally made sure that she received just compensation for her performance.

Pre-performance anxiety in the days before Thanksgiving usually raised the stress level in the Crocker household and, with it, the amount of bickering and the number of sharp comments exchanged. This year, however, Bill was in a generous and cheerful spirit in the week leading up to Thanksgiving. This deviation from the usual sentiments of the season initially caught Sally off guard. She became suspicious. She thought back to the last Thanksgiving they hosted when Bill worked for the National Tobacco Institute. His good mood in the days leading up to that Thanksgiving abruptly switched when one of their guests, his pretty young assistant, left in tears toward the end of the meal for no apparent reason, or at least not for a reason that Sally wanted to consider. But she detected no telltale signs of a similar situation this year. Instead, she noted Bill's frequent self-congratulatory comments over breakfast ("You should have heard how I spun this story to a reporter yesterday"), and she concluded there was a much more benign source of his current good humor.

The positive early responses to Fox's paper, or more precisely, Crocker's interpretation of that paper, showed up in articles in *The Savior Sentinel*, *One Way Weekly*, and *Good News!* Each of these publications, following Crocker's suggestion, prominently mentioned CROSS's sponsorship of Fox's research. The authors of these articles were also kind enough to use (or were so caught up with other things that they found it easiest to take) verbatim, language from Crocker's press release. And, more recently, the mainstream media had even started to show some interest. Daily papers in Texas, Virginia, Ohio, and Florida (papers where he had old friends from his tobacco days) mentioned the story. More important, an article appeared in *USA Today* mentioning "research by Professor David Fox, which was sponsored by the Center to Research Opportunities for a Spiritual Society" in a short article "Abstinence Programs Show Good Results" on page 5.

Crocker made sure that the trustees of CROSS saw these news clippings. But it wasn't just these placements that cheered him; he knew from his long experience in the public relations industry that, once a story like this got some traction, it could get real legs. After all, sex sells, and teen sex sells even better. Discretion may be the better part of valor, but it is the lesser part of sales; just ask any advertising executive, television producer, music executive, or movie mogul. With profits on one side, and the word of God on the other, teenage sexual activity was sure to be the site of trench cultural warfare for a long time. And with the publicity he was generating with the most recent *CROSS Currents* working paper, Crocker foresaw his promotion to a major's rank in these culture wars.

He anticipated this promotion partly because of the initial coverage of the Fox article but, even more so, because his own general, Bob Dronin, was beginning to show him favor. Dronin had accepted Bill and Sally's holiday invitation this year. It was the first time he had accepted any type of invitation from the Crockers. Up until now, Dronin graciously declined any and all invitations, saying that other obligations prevented him from attending their

Thanksgiving dinner, Fourth of July picnic, or Memorial Day cookout. But this year, after initially declining the Thanksgiving invitation, Dronin called back a few days before the holiday to tell Bill and Sally he would be happy to join them. He also mentioned, in that phone conversation, how his friends had been calling him about the "fine work that CROSS has been doing, especially this stuff on teenage abstinence." The central goal of CROSS was, of course, to shift the public debate, but if it also served to improve Bob Dronin's standing among his friends, well, that was another good reason for him to donate generously.

Crocker had already invited two trustees and their spouses to Thanksgiving, Louise Parsons, and Reverend Warren Thomas. Louise Parsons was particularly interested in how CROSS could stem the tide of moral pollution found in the media and on the Internet, especially videos that linked music with lurid images of teenagers and young adults doing the most ungodly things. She was a big fan of teenage abstinence programs (which, she frequently said, moved teenagers "nearer to God and further from Hollywood"). It was especially fortunate that her moral fervor was matched by her husband Henry's business success, and his willingness to fund his wife's crusades (which, he often mentioned, kept her "nearer to God and further from me").

Reverend Thomas had a different focus, the teaching of the false doctrine of evolution in the schools. He was particularly pleased with the *CROSS Currents* working paper that showed teaching evolution had no positive effect on SAT scores. He was disappointed, however, that this pathbreaking research did not attract more public attention, a point he raised often in the privacy of his home with his wife Constance. But, anxious to be a good team player, the reverend wanted to make it clear during Thanksgiving that he was happy that this research on teenage abstinence was finally putting CROSS on the map.

The good reverend would be given an opportunity to make this point at the beginning of the Thanksgiving dinner since Sally had phoned to ask him to say grace before the meal. She oversaw all the other preparations as well, including the seating plan (Bill at the head of the table, with Dronin on his right and Louise Parsons on his left), the menu (traditional, but of a quality befitting the importance of the guests), and the decorations (a cornucopia centerpiece and autumnal colors). Bill was happy to cede these womanly tasks to her, though he did request that each place setting include a booklet with copies of all the newspaper articles that mentioned "Something for Nothing" that he had just printed. After some discussion on the appropriateness of such a blatant (and, according to Sally, gauche) effort at self-promotion, a compromise was reached; the booklets could be placed next to each dinner plate, but each one needed to include a sticker of a turkey and a Pilgrim father on its cover.

There wasn't much left of the turkey, or of the chestnut stuffing, au gratin potatoes, asparagus, candied yams, or cranberry sauce. Bill, Sally, and their guests pushed away from the table, all agreeing they were too full for dessert, at least just then. Sally told the help to clear, and, in a little while, to serve coffee in the living room. There would be enough time later for the pumpkin pies, apple pies, peach pies, and seven-layer cakes.

"The Lord's bounty is plentiful this year," commented Reverend Thomas as he sank back into the cushions of the couch.

"Amen," intoned Mrs. Thomas, who could always be counted on to provide the appropriate congregational response.

"A fine spread, Sally, a fine spread," said Bob Dronin as he sat in a wingback chair opposite the fireplace.

"Why thank you, Bob," replied Sally, who could rightly take credit for her organizational abilities but was also willing to take the statement as a compliment for her culinary skills, although these had not been on display.

"And a nice little party favor to go with the meal," said Dronin, who held up the booklet with the news clippings that he had brought with him from the table.

Crocker had also brought the booklet with him from the table, and glanced demurely at the floor as he answered, "Just trying to do the Lord's Will, Bob."

Louise Parsons said, "I just glanced at this book, Bill, but it looks like CROSS is getting some good coverage about these abstinence programs. Young people today need to know that there are alternatives, and good for you to show that there are rewards for acting in a Christian way."

"I am so pleased that CROSS is getting the attention it deserves," added Reverend Thomas.

"Who is this Fox fellow?" Henry Parsons asked. "He's not a professor at SAVE, is he?"

"Professor David Fox is an up-and-coming young academic star," Crocker answered with a glance at Parsons and a longer look at Bob Dronin. "He is doing some of the most important research on social issues of any economist his age. We believe that our first collaboration with him, as important as it is, is just the beginning of a long and productive relationship."

"That's just the type of development that CROSS needs," proclaimed Dronin. "You are doing a fine job of leveraging, Bill. My friends in Dallas and Tallahassee have mentioned that they are seeing CROSS mentioned in their newspapers. Publicity like this can only be good for us, for all of us."

"We should get young professors like him to address our youth group conventions," suggested Reverend Thomas. "Our teenagers need role models of all types, including professors, and especially ones with such an important and uplifting message."

Louise asked, "Does this Professor Fox belong to one of our affiliated congregations?"

"I believe he is a Baptist," answered Crocker, taking a cup of coffee from the tray offered to him by the hired help.

Chapter 16

David had successfully negotiated a one-day visit with his parents during the Thanksgiving holiday, despite their initial efforts to get him to stay from Wednesday night until Sunday afternoon. The deal agreed to by the parties stipulated that David Fox would leave Knittersville early on Thursday morning and drive directly to the residence of his parents, Harry and Ruth Fox, in the suburbs of Boston, arriving well before dinner was scheduled to be served at 2:00. David would stay over in "his" room on Thursday night, a room that, in fact, had long since been made into a TV den with a pullout couch. He would then return to Kester on Friday ("But not so early, right?" his mother asked). In the past, his negotiation had not been nearly as successful, and the best he had done was a two-night stay. This year, however, arguments about the demands facing a new professor won the day (the day, in this case, being Friday rather than Sunday).

David's claim that work demands only allowed him a short stay were both convenient and closer to the truth than most of the claims he had made in his past efforts to negotiate time spent with family. Since the midterm break in October, he had found it a struggle to keep his class preparations comfortably ahead of his class presentations. The prospect of running out of material mid-class forced him to use some of his Tuesday and Thursday mornings to prepare lectures rather than work on research. In one way, this was fine; time spent on class preparation always yielded results while time spent on research often seemed to accomplish little. But journal articles, or at least the research papers that were their precursors, were his ticket to a tenure-track job.

Another reason for him to return early to Knittersville was to see Angie. Overall, he thought their relationship was going, well, swimmingly. After that first time they made love, David was thrilled that he was with a woman, especially one as pretty as Angie. Since then, while his appreciation of her beauty remained strong, he also became more and more enamored with her sense of humor, her good sense about practical matters, and her kindness—though, he had to admit to himself, he wasn't sure if a funny, sensible, kind, but unattractive woman would have captured his heart the way Angie did.

His favorite times with her were the evenings they stayed in and cooked dinner together. They would meet at the grocery store, selecting ingredients for that evening's feast. The first time they did this, David spent a half hour searching the Internet for recipes and printed one out to bring with him to the market. Angie looked at the recipe and crumpled it up. "David, I've spent my whole life cooking and watching my mother cook. I don't need some web-based plan for dinner." He then followed her as she walked up and down the aisles, selecting cans of tomato paste, red and green peppers, fresh garlic, and chicken breasts, seemingly at random.

"You don't have any spices in your apartment, do you?" she asked with a smile.

"I've got salt. And pepper, too."

"Salt's not a spice."

"It is so. It's the Jewish spice."

Angie laughed, but then led David to the spice section where she picked out six different spices. She guided David to the bakery aisle, picked up a fresh baguette, and broke off the end, giving a piece to David and then taking a piece for herself.

When they got ready to check out, Angie told the woman working the register, "Mrs. Cassaro, how can your store sell this bread? Look, the end is missing. I think we should get a discount." Angie's argument would have been more convincing had she already swallowed the piece of bread she was eating. Mrs. Cassaro, used to these kinds of pranks from someone she watched grow up, said, "Angelica, didn't your mother teach you not to speak with your mouth full? Besides, I think it was you who broke that bread." Angie, with a mock look of surprise, replied, "Hey, I'm not into pointing fingers here."

Mrs. Cassaro joined David in laughing at this. David guessed that, later that evening, Mrs. Cassaro would phone Giovanna to tell her about Angelica standing in the checkout line, arm in arm with a boy from out of town. But of course, Giovanna already knew about David. Judging by the size of the salads he was served in the cafeteria, she seemed to accept her daughter's relationship with him, as long as it was what Angie wanted.

And it did seem to be what Angie wanted, at least most of the time. But there were a couple of times when he wondered about that. There had been that fight a few weeks ago, the Saturday night after they got back from Albany. They were all in a bad mood that day after they left Capital Letters. He and Jeff grew quiet, thinking about what happens if you don't get a tenure-track job, or, even if you do, if you don't get tenure. Angie was testy, no doubt still smarting from Van Ronan's surprise when he learned she was a Knittersville townie. Later that night, after they dropped Jeff off, David mentioned he had a lot to do the next day.

"You always complain about being so busy. Christ, you teach, what, five or six hours a week?"

"Yeah, but for every hour in the classroom I spend three or four preparing."

"Okay, David, I can do math too. That means you spend about thirty hours a week at work, tops. I usually work forty-five or fifty hours, especially when I'm traveling, and I'm not constantly bitching about how much I have to do."

"That's only the teaching. I've also got to spend time trying to finish my research, otherwise I'm fucked."

She grew quiet. David had explained to her how academic jobs depend upon research, using Minard's metaphor of the coin of the realm.

"I'm sorry, that was mean. I know you're working hard and under a lot of pressure."

"That's okay. I know I was distracted today."

They spent that evening together. The next morning, David tried his best to avoid thinking about his work and to stay engaged with Angie when they ate breakfast together. When they finished breakfast, she told him that she would clean up the dishes and then get going so he could do his work. Later that day, she surprised him by coming back to his apartment with sandwiches from a deli in town. "I figured you didn't take time for lunch, and you've got to keep your strength up." Of course, making love right after lunch did little to help David keep his strength up, but it did help put him in a much better mood.

Things continued to go well up until last Monday, just before the Thanksgiving break. They had arranged to meet at the grocery store to buy food for dinner, but he was a half hour late. He had been meeting with Jenny Lake, who stopped by unexpectedly to discuss her thesis since she was leaving town the next day and would not be available for their regular Wednesday meeting. David was impressed by Jenny's progress. After a while, the discussion moved from her thesis to her plans after graduation. David lost track of time and, before he knew it, an hour had passed. When he saw the time, he jumped up and, while putting on his coat, told Jenny he was late for an appointment. She stood up, apologized for making him late, and then gave him a hug and wished him a happy holiday. The hug seemed to have left the imprint of her body on him. He felt that imprint during the entire trip from his office to the market.

Angie was angry when he met her, and, rightly so, he thought. He apologized. She asked him why he was so late, and he mumbled something about a lot of students during his office hours, this being a short week and all. She looked at him for a moment, as if she was waiting for him to say something else, but he just started down the aisle looking for pasta sauce and, after a moment, she fell in step behind him. He had the sense that she continued to look at him in a searching way as they finished the shopping. At the checkout counter, she asked him, "David, is there anything you want to tell me?"

"Uh, I'm really sorry about being so late."

"Anything else?"

"I'm really, really sorry?"

She looked at him for a moment, but then just said, "Forget about it," and turned to get her money out of her pocketbook. It didn't seem as if she had forgotten about it, though, at least while they walked to his apartment, or as they began to cook. But, gradually, they began to chat while preparing the food, as they always did, and by time they sat down to eat things had gotten back to normal.

Back to normal? Can you really call it "back to normal" after only a month of being together? Had it really been only a month?

Maybe it seemed like more because, since that first night together, Angie was never very far from his thoughts, even when they had not seen each other for a few days because of her travels.

But since it had been only a month, he could, with good conscience, evade any discussion of this relationship with his parents and relatives during Thanksgiving. Why ruin their dinner by mentioning he was in love with a Catholic girl from Knittersville? If he and Angie were still going strong in December, he could tell them then. The announcement to his family could be a sort of Christmas gift.

There wasn't much left of the turkey, or of the stuffing, the green beans, the latkes, or the applesauce left on the table by the end of the meal. As in years past, David found the turkey a bit dry and the green beans a little limp, but the latkes were just right. Serving latkes at Thanksgiving was a tradition in the Fox household. David had always thought of this tradition as his family's way to herald in the upcoming Chanukah season, just as the Christmas lights that appeared in the commercial district of town on the day before Thanksgiving was a signal to his gentile friends of the advent of their upcoming frantic shopping period.

David's new job was the subject of the first few minutes of the dinner conversation. He tried to explain how, as a professor, he was expected to spend most of his time doing research and publishing from his dissertation. He had more luck explaining national income accounting to freshman.

"So are you saying that a college teacher spends only five hours a week teaching?" his mother asked.

"Yeah, but there's a lot of prep time."

"You mean for your lesson plans?"

"Not lesson plans, Ma, lecture preparation. For every hour in the classroom, I have to spend about five hours preparing." He was worried that, like Angie, his relatives could do the math.

They could.

"How are you so busy, then?" his father asked.

"Remember how I was working full-time on my dissertation?"

"Who could forget?" his mother quickly interjected.

David carried on as if she had not said anything, a skill passed down from generation to generation, in this case, from father to son. "Now it's like I'm doing all that teaching and also working on my dissertation. Except it's not the dissertation, it's articles from the dissertation that I'm trying to get published."

"What kind of magazine publishes these articles?" his grandfather asked.

"Journals, not magazines, Zaydie. They're scholarly journals. You send your article in, and they send it to other professors who review it. If they like it enough, you get a chance to revise it, and then send it in again. Eventually, hopefully, they publish it."

"Why don't you just send it to a real magazine and be done with it?"

"Real magazines don't publish these kinds of articles, Zaydie. Real magazines publish articles that people like to read."

There was a collective sense of bewilderment at this; why spend all your time writing articles that were only reluctantly accepted for magazines that people didn't want to read? And for a job that really didn't pay that well and kept you in some little *nebishe* town? Retail made so much more sense than college teaching.

Fortunately, the conversation soon turned to its usual topics: the sad state of the world, the precarious state of business, and, most important, the ill state of health suffered by friends and relatives.

David found it easy to remove himself from these conversations, with only the occasional mumbled agreement required from him.

After dinner, he helped his mother and his aunt clear the table and fill the dishwasher. The three of them then joined his father, his uncle, and his grandfather in the living room. In an hour or two, his mother would put out the leftover turkey on platters, along with loaves of rye bread and Russian dressing, so everyone could make sandwiches. In the meantime, they could all have some quality family time during which the shortcomings of relatives who were not present could be discussed.

David's grandfather caught him looking at his watch after only ten minutes in the living room. "So, Davie, these articles of yours, what're they about?" he asked, trying to draw him into the conversation.

He had been strategizing about his job applications and, in particular, about whether and how to mention his burgeoning notoriety due to his working paper with CROSS, when his grandfather posed his question. So, rather than talk about his dissertation work, he answered his grandfather by saying, "Actually, Zaydie, my research shows the positive effects of teenage abstinence programs."

"What are you talking about?" David's father asked. "I don't remember that your dissertation was about that."

Harry Fox probably did not recall the exact subject of his son's dissertation, but he was pretty certain it didn't have anything to do with sex—or even a lack of sex. That he would have remembered.

"It's not actually my dissertation, Dad, it's some other research I did."

"So David, you do have time to get some new research done," his aunt said, showing that she had paid a lot more attention to his comments at the dinner table than she let on at the time.

"Aunt Sarah, this is some other work that I did when I was in graduate school. In fact, there was a newspaper article about my research in *USA Today*."

He immediately regretted mentioning this.

"*USA Today*!" his grandfather said. "Harry, why didn't you tell me about this?"

"Who knew?" said Harry. "David, why didn't you tell us? We could have shown everyone!"

"It wasn't that big a deal," David replied.

"Not a big deal?" replied his mother. "David, people in hotels all over the country read *USA Today*."

David's grandfather looked a little puzzled. "Davie, how did they find out about your research? You said you were so worried about publishing. Did you publish this research already?"

"No, Zaydie, this group publicized my work."

"What group?" his uncle asked.

He chose his words carefully. "Uncle Bernie, it's a group that wants to promote teenage abstinence programs."

"Like a church?" asked his aunt Sarah.

"Not exactly a church."

"How much is it not exactly a church?" asked his father.

"It's this group in Virginia, the Center to Research Opportunities for Society. It's really pretty much cross-denominational. I guess that's why it's called CROSS."

"Davie, you're working for a group called CROSS? In Virginia?"

"No, Zaydie, I'm not working for them, they're just interested in my research and want to publish it."

"Are they paying you?" his aunt Sarah asked.

"A little."

"Oy, Davie, is this so smart to do?"

"Dad, I'm sure David knows what he's doing," said Ruth. "David, you do know what you're doing, don't you?"

In all truthfulness, David did not know what he was doing, and that was what he was thinking about when his grandfather first asked him about his research. He welcomed the attention that his research had been getting in *USA Today* and in the local papers that Crocker had sent him. But he was becoming concerned about how the colleges he was applying to would view this work, and especially what search committees would think if they found out that his work was being promoted by a group called CROSS. David knew about the liberal bias of college hiring committees—in fact, he shared it. He came by his liberal bias honestly, having had it developed right here in this room with these relatives. But while their politics made sense to him, they didn't really understand academia, or what it takes to get a tenure-track job. So he was not sure about what he was doing, but he was certain that fate had handed him a chance, one that he shouldn't pass up, even if it was making for some strange bedfellows.

"It's a good opportunity to get my research noticed, Ma. And none of you have to worry. It's not like I joined a church or anything. It's just a research organization."

"I worry about you out there in the sticks," said David's father. "It's too bad you couldn't get a job around here, or in New York."

Harry's statement reflected a father's concern and love and was not at all an effort to pass harsh judgment on David's success to date. Harry just did not realize how difficult it was to get an academic job in a major metropolitan area. Even though this statement was not meant to be hurtful, he would have felt wounded by it a few weeks ago. Its effect on this holiday, however, was greatly mitigated because, while Knittersville did not have theaters, or clubs, or even good bookstores, Boston did not have Angie.

Chapter 17

David had not planned to work on Friday afternoon or on Saturday, despite the reason he had given his parents for departing early. In fact, his main motivation for returning to Knittersville, the one he did not share with his parents, was foremost on his mind as he got on the Massachusetts Turnpike on Friday morning. He called Angie as he began to drive west to arrange to meet her for a drink at the Cask and Barrel when he returned to town. Much to his dismay, Angie was unexpectedly tied up with her family. She asked if he would like to come over to her mother's house to meet her aunts, uncles, and cousins, but, having had his fill of both food and family, he begged off. Instead, they arranged to meet on Saturday night for dinner, when Angie could get away.

David thought about calling Jeff, but then remembered that he was with his relatives in New Jersey until Sunday. So it looked as if he would be on his own from Friday afternoon until he met Angie on Saturday night. Circumstances were making an honest man out of him; he would get right to work once he returned to his apartment, just as he had told his parents he would.

It was late afternoon when he rolled into Knittersville. The pallid light of the sun muted the colors in the town. In four hours he had traveled from the Boston suburb where his parents lived to the town he now called home. The contrast between the two places was striking and a little disorienting. Did Knittersville seem poorer today than when he'd left the previous morning? Had the houses really become more worn down overnight? Were there this many shuttered shops on Main Street yesterday? Was it the Christmas lights strung across front porches and in the windows of the stores that presented a contrast he had not noticed before? Or was it the leaden skies and the bare tree branches, harbingers of the coming long winter, that contributed to the general feeling of a town that had seen better days?

The long car trip, this sense of disorientation, and the disappointment in not seeing Angie put him in a somber mood. David entered his apartment and could not help but compare its meager dimensions to the much larger layout of his parents' house. He suddenly didn't feel like getting to work on revising his papers or preparing for next week's classes. He paced around for a minute with his coat on and his keys still in his hand. A long swim would have helped, but the Weissmüller Pool was closed until Monday. A solo visit to the Cask and Barrel was out of the question since that would have been an admission, to both himself and the rest of the world, that things were not going well. So rather than wallow in the present, he would take charge of the future. He hung up his coat, put down his keys, and got a beer out of the refrigerator. He sat down in front of his computer, and, as soon as it booted up, logged onto the Internet site Job Openings for Economists.

The Job Openings for Economists website had replaced the monthly mailings of the same name that the American Economic Association had published since the middle of the twentieth century. The advantage of the website over the old hardcopy mailings was that jobs could be posted every day rather than once per month. The disadvantage of the website was that jobs could be posted every day rather than once per month, and, for that reason, people like David, who were searching for a job, spent an inordinate amount of time in October and November logging onto and searching the website.

Although David had been checking out the website on a regular basis, he had not yet found the time, or the energy, to get serious about the job search and use the information that was posted. But the deadline for applications was approaching and now, having returned to Knittersville, he felt motivated to do something. He got a pad of paper and, as he scrolled through Job Openings for Economists, began to write down the colleges and universities that might be interested in hiring a relatively fresh PhD from an Ivy League university who had a year of teaching experience and increasingly modest expectations.

"I can't believe you actually enjoyed being with your family on Thanksgiving," David said to Angie after the waiter took their order. She looked particularly pretty this evening in the subdued light of the booth. Being apart for a few days, a common experience given her work travel, always made him appreciate her more. This effect was heightened this evening by the way he had spent the days apart; first with his family, and then working on application letters and materials to be sent with the applications.

"My cousins are like brothers and sisters to me; we grew up together. I was always visiting my aunts and uncles when I was a kid. Why didn't you want to come over to meet them?"

This was, in fact, a good question, one that he himself had pondered. He loved to be with Angie and felt pretty comfortable with Giovanna. But meeting the whole family seemed like a big step, and one that would lead to entanglements; her cousins Tony and Vinny might want to hang out and watch sports on TV, and her uncle Sal might offer him a job. There would be questions about his intentions, his prospects, and his family. And, speaking of his family, Angie might expect a reciprocal invitation. No, for now at least, dinner for two suited him fine.

"I would've come over, but I've got to get my applications sent out."

"You couldn't have taken some time out from that?"

"The deadlines for submitting the materials are this week."

Angie seemed a little exasperated, but he saw she made an effort to become reengaged with this line of conversation. "How's it going so far?" she asked.

"Okay, but it seems like such a crapshoot. There are a lot of qualified people for each job, so I don't know how they decide on the fifteen they interview at the meetings."

"What meetings?"

He remembered that not everyone was familiar with the brutal manner that his profession had devised for allocating scarce jobs. Having been through the process once already, he did not look forward to beginning it again. Last year, he began the process just before Thanksgiving, with high hopes, hopes that in the end were left unfulfilled. He had learned that he was the second choice for at least two jobs, but unlike horse racing, you get no credit for place or show in this derby.

"Schools advertise online for professors during the fall. Usually the job descriptions are broad enough so that a school will get 150 applications for a single position. But also, everyone applies for everything since you might get lucky."

"Those are pretty long odds."

"Tell me about it. Out of those 150, each school selects about 15 applicants to interview at the annual economics convention in early January. Last year, I got lucky, I had ten interviews. My main qualifications that set me apart from the pack seemed to be a degree from Columbia and being a native English speaker."

"What are those interviews like?"

"It's awful. The first big challenge is to get to the hotel room for your interview. All the interviews start on the hour, which means that about a thousand desperate applicants are all trying to use the same elevator bank at ten minutes before the hour. Last time, I resorted to the stairwell, which was fine when I had to get from the tenth floor to the fifth floor, but wasn't so great when, an hour later, I had to go back up to the thirteenth floor in less than ten minutes. It's hard to make a good first impression when you're sweaty and out-of-breath."

"You made a pretty good first impression on me even though you were out of breath."

"That's because I was wearing my bathing suit, not my business suit. And I didn't start talking to you immediately about my dissertation, which is what they always ask you as soon as you sit down. And you didn't start aggressively questioning my methodology or my data, which is how interviewers show interest."

"But we did race pretty aggressively that first time."

"I didn't think it was a competition, remember?"

"Yes you did. You think everything's a competition."

"Maybe. But getting a job is, for sure."

"So what happens after these hotel room interviews?"

"The colleges will invite three or four people to come for a one-day visit. It's called a 'fly-out,' which is unfortunate given the meaning of the term in baseball. When you go to these schools, you give a talk, you meet with lots of the professors and with some students, and also you meet with a dean. It's pretty high stress, you have to be on and enthusiastic for everyone."

"Enthusiasm is not your strong suit," Angie offered.

"Hey, I'm enthusiastic about you, aren't I?"

"Mostly, I guess. Are you enthusiastic enough about me to stay at Kester for another year?"

"Angie, if I can get a tenure-track job here it would be great, but it's a long shot here, and everywhere else. My goal has to be to get a tenure-track job. I don't want to just keep stringing together these one-year appointments."

"How important is it to you to stay at Kester?"

"What's really important is that I get a tenure-track job anywhere."

She stared at him for a moment and raised her eyebrows. He realized how this last comment sounded, but he was also trying to be realistic and honest with her. It was the only fair thing to do. He had spent the last two days responding to advertisements for jobs all over the country. Sure, he would like to get a job where they could still see each other, one not too far away, but he might only get one offer and it could be on the West Coast.

After a moment or two of silence between them, Angie took a sudden interest in the wine left in her glass and began to swirl it around. Just then, the waiter came with their dinners. The two of them ate in silence for a while.

As he picked at his food, David thought that they might not even be together next year. No, that wasn't an outcome he wanted to think about, not now. Last year didn't work out, but there's no reason not to be more hopeful this time around. He had more things going for him now than he did a year ago; a completed dissertation, teaching experience, research that was under way. And other things that set him apart.

"You know, I have been thinking about it and I can use this article that CROSS is publicizing to help me at least get some first interviews."

"David, from what you tell me, that director of CROSS seems a little creepy. You don't even like that article you wrote about abstinence. Didn't you tell me you thought it was a kind of joke?"

"Well sure, at first I didn't take it very seriously. But people seem interested in it—it's like this *Freakonomics* thing, but even better because it's about sex."

"It's about not having sex," Angie corrected him.

"Sex, not sex, what's the difference. The main thing is to get noticed."

They finished the meals, and David signaled to the waiter for the check. He was getting tired of talking about his job search, especially after Angie questioned his reliance on using the publicity for "Something for Nothing" to his advantage, a point he had debated with himself on the drive from Boston and thought he had resolved.

The waiter brought the check. As he and Angie got out their money to pay, he asked her, "So, you want to come over tonight?"

"David, I really should get back to my family tonight. My cousins from New York are leaving early tomorrow morning."

The look of disappointment on his face must have been pretty clear to Angie.

"It's like you said, David, sex, not sex, what's the difference?"

Kester College
Economics Department
Knittersville, New York 12078

November 25, 2007

Search Committee
Department of Economics
Brunsfield College
Louistown, Maine 01132

To the Search Committee:

I would like to apply for the assistant professor position that you advertised in the October issue of *Job Openings for Economists*. As indicated in the enclosed CV, I received my PhD from Columbia University in May 2007. This year I am a visiting professor at Kester College where I am teaching Principles of Economics and The Economics of Social Issues.

My research is in the area of empirical analyses of public policy programs. The enclosed chapter from my dissertation considers the effects of recycling programs on consumption. I plan to submit a version of this chapter to a journal within the next few weeks. I should also mention that another research paper of mine, on the effects of school-based behavior modification programs in Kentucky, has been published as a working paper and has been getting some attention in the popular press. Enclosed is a recent clipping from *USA Today*.

I am interested in a tenure-track position at a school that values teaching as well as research. My experience at Kester has allowed me to hone my teaching skills and expand my portfolio of courses. I will be attending the Allied Social Sciences Association convention in Boston in early January and will be available for interviews at that time.

Thank you for considering my application.

Sincerely,
David Fox
Visiting Assistant Professor

Chapter 18

David awoke on the Monday after the Thanksgiving break to find four inches of freshly fallen snow covering Knittersville. Snow-flakes had been in the air earlier in November, but, up until this storm, there was nothing more than a light dusting that melted on the roads as soon as it alighted. This was different. The snow on the ground this morning would remain until March. This snowfall shifted the season, overnight, from autumn to winter.

But it did not take a coating of snow to make the first day of classes after Thanksgiving seem like the beginning of a new season for the students of Kester College. After the long holiday weekend, there were only five classes left for each of the fall semester courses. For those students who were concerned about their grades, mainly because Kester was, for them, a way station to an MBA, an MD, or a JD, there would be no days off during the three weeks between the end of the Thanksgiving holiday and final exams. The library opened for extended hours, all-night study rooms were made available in the student union, and resident assistants stocked the common rooms in dormitories with donuts, juice, and coffee in the evenings. Class notes would be reviewed, outlines would be written, and practice exams would be taken. There would also be a run on caffeine pills in the pharmacy near campus.

The change in the season was also apparent to the faculty as November drew to a close. Professors had to determine how much was left to cover in the remaining classes. The last five classes would be crammed with material if professors spent too much time in September and October pandering to students' needs to make their views known. Time would also be tight if professors indulged their own desires to share political opinions, personal reflections, and witty asides. The personal bond professors thought they had forged with their students during those leisurely pre-Thanksgiving classes would be broken in the hectic rush after the holiday. As unfair as it seemed to professors, this would adversely affect evaluations written by students with short memories and long hopes for their own academic success. Professors facing the other situation, with too little material left to share with their students, could be luckier if their shortfall was on the order of one class or so. In this case, it was common to magnanimously offer to devote the last class to students' questions and review. Students always mistakenly thought this offer was extended for their benefit.

David happily found himself with not too much material, not too little material, but just the right amount, as he sat in his office on the Monday after Thanksgiving and looked over his notes for his remaining classes. Despite what he had told his parents and, in fact, what he himself had believed until he actually reviewed his notes, he needed only to touch up a few lectures in order to close out the semester. Writing two finals was, of course, another matter. He also knew that there was almost a full week's worth of grading waiting for him in December. Still, he had a bit more time to devote to the job application process than he had anticipated.

There were still about fifteen minutes left until his class was to begin when David's office phone rang.

"Hello?"

A woman's voice answered, one that enunciated well and contained a hint of the South. "Professor David Fox, please."

"This is Professor Fox."

"Please hold for a call from Dr. William Crocker, director of CROSS."

In five seconds, too little time for David to overcome his surprise at receiving this call, or to think about what he should say, he heard a man's deep voice, a voice that would seem at home in an exclusive men's club in Louisville or Atlanta, say, "David, Bill Crocker. It's a pleasure to finally get a chance to speak with you."

"Hi, how are you?" was the best he could come up with as a reply.

"David, I'm just fine. I hope I'm not catching you at an inconvenient time."

"Well, I have to teach pretty soon, but I have a few minutes now."

"That's great. I'll take only a minute of your valuable time. We here at CROSS are very excited about your work, as you know from our correspondence. We have been successful, very successful, in getting the media interested in your work as well."

"I know. I saw the article in *USA Today*. Thanks a lot for promoting my work."

"That's what we do here, support and spread the work of scholars like you. I wanted to let you know that Alan Glidden wants to interview you on his radio show."

"Alan Glidden?"

"David, Alan Glidden has one of the most popular talk radio shows in the country, *Talk Right*. You are familiar with it, aren't you?"

"I've heard of him, but I don't get a chance to listen to talk radio very often."

"Of course not. I can fully understand how your research takes up your time. But we here at CROSS think that you could do both us and yourself a favor by spending a few minutes with Alan. He wants to ask you about 'Something for Nothing' and get the word out about this important contribution."

He felt a tightening in his chest. He knew that none of his friends or family would listen to a show like *Talk Right*, but, nevertheless, he was nervous about going on national radio, especially to talk about "Something for Nothing." Somebody listened to that show, actually a lot of somebodies, even if they weren't the people with whom he worked, drank, played, or attended religious services.

Crocker, not hearing a response, added, "This is a wonderful opportunity for you to get your research noticed, to help make your name."

He thought about the stack of application letters he was about to post that day. "Okay, fine. Do you know which week they want to talk with me?"

"David, this is radio, not an encyclopedia. They want you on the show today."

"Today?"

"Yes, for the 5:00 show. You are available then, aren't you?"

"Well, yeah, I guess so."

"Great, I'll contact June Pendleton who is the producer of the show. She'll give you a call around 4:45 at this number, and prep you for the show. You're the second story today, and your segment will start at 5:15."

"How will we get a chance to record ten minutes of material if we start at 4:45?"

"David, this is live radio. You'll love it. I'll be listening in, as will all of us here at CROSS. Good luck, son."

With that, Crocker hung up. David stared at the phone for a few seconds before he replaced the handset in the cradle. He tried to allay his concerns and anxiety by thinking about the positive aspects of the upcoming radio interview, but all he could come up with was that he wouldn't have to worry about what to wear.

David decided against telling anyone about the radio interview. His parents, had they known, would drop everything to search the dial for the Boston station that carried the show. They would make sure that they, and a recording device, and all their friends, were by the radio at 5:00. But he was afraid that their worst suspicions about CROSS would only be realized if they listened to him speaking with Alan Glidden. He also guessed that Jeff might be familiar with Glidden, if only because he was the type of talk show host who regularly railed against the gay liberal agenda and its corrosive effects on the moral fiber of America. Angie had already called Crocker "a creep," so there was no need to help fuel her concerns about his relationship with CROSS either. In fact, David hoped that no one he knew, or would ever meet, would be listening. Based on what he knew about the show, and guessed about its audience, he thought this hope was reasonable.

David was back at his desk by 3:45 after his class ended, and he began to take notes to refresh his memory about his paper on teenage abstinence. He tried to think of ways to explain what he had estimated, and what inferences could and could not be drawn from his results. But, in his extremely limited efforts to explain his research ideas to noneconomists (that is, his parents or, more recently, Angie), he knew that it was difficult to convey anything but the most cursory view of his work.

His phone rang at precisely 4:45.

"Hello?"

"David Fox?" said a very professional sounding women's voice.

"Yes?"

"Good afternoon, Professor Fox. This is June Pendleton with *Talk Right*. Thank you for agreeing to be on the show today."

"Glad to help out."

"Now I imagine you do this type of thing all the time, so . . ."

"Actually, this is my first time on live radio."

There was a short pause on the other end of the line.

"Well, I'm sure you'll do fine. A few ground rules. Don't interrupt Mr. Glidden when he is asking a question. Try to keep your answers short, but not too short. Avoid technical jargon; remember our audience is just ordinary folks. And don't try to be funny; it never works."

"Sure, okay, I won't be funny."

"Now your research shows that teenage abstinence programs are good, correct?"

"Well, actually, what my research shows is that in a trial program in Kentucky there was evidence that the schools that had these programs, as compared to a control group, had . . ."

June's voice conveyed the tiniest bit of impatience. "Professor Fox, does your research show that teenage abstinence programs are good?"

"Yes, I suppose it does."

"You suppose it does, or it does?"

"It does. My research shows that there are some really positive effects of teenage abstinence programs."

"Good, very good. And therefore, in general, the teaching of values in our public school system should be encouraged."

"Well, you know, my research was only about this one specific program in one state and it's hard to generalize from . . ."

The level of impatience in June's voice notched up. "Professor Fox, does your research show that values education is important?"

"I suppose, er, yes, it does."

"Fine. You'll do great on the show, I'm sure. I'm going to hang up now. My assistant will call you at 5:10, and you'll start your interview with Mr. Glidden at 5:15. He'll speak with you for about four minutes, and then you and he will field some calls from listeners for the final three minutes of your segment."

"Calls from listeners?" David asked.

"Yes, you'll do great. I need to hang up now. Best of luck. Goodbye."

For the second time that day, David found himself staring at the phone before replacing the handset in the cradle.

Transcript of *Talk Right*

Monday, November 26, 2007: Segment 2: 5:15–5:23 EST

AG We're back. Welcome again to *Talk Right*. My listeners, the *Talk Right* Rebels, know that the real climate crisis in this country has to do with the moral climate. Moral global warming is taking place because our so-called leaders are too influenced by the liberals in the media to take action and stop the slide toward sexual promiscuity and gay marriage. In this segment, we are speaking with Professor David Fox of Kester College in New York State. Professor Fox, who works with our friends at CROSS, that's the Center to Research Opportunities for a Spiritual Society, has shown that teenage abstinence programs work, and they work well. Welcome to *Talk Right,* Professor Fox.

DF Thank you, Alan.

AG Professor Fox, your research studies an innovative teenage abstinence program in our great state of Kentucky, is that right?

DF Yes, Alan, there was a program there to teach abstinence to ninth and tenth graders. Students were then surveyed when they were juniors and seniors.

AG And these programs worked, right Professor?

DF Well, yes, there is some evidence that teenage pregnancy rates fell.

AG These programs teach students to respect their bodies and themselves, don't they?

DF Something is going on to help these kids, Alan.

AG Well said, Professor, something is going on to help these kids. And helping kids is what it should be all about, isn't it? The effect you find is important, Professor, and you even write that it is highly significant.

DF Significant in this case, Alan, means statistically significant. What you want to do is to test whether the coefficients . . .

AG Yes, folks, statistics show that this program works and that it is important for our nation in these times of moral slippage. In fact, Professor, don't you show that it wasn't only pregnancy rates that were affected? Why don't you tell the *Talk Right Rebels* who are listening what else you found?

DF   The study also looks at instances of handguns brought to school, and of grades on standardized tests. The teenage abstinence program was associated with fewer handguns being brought to school and better grades on tests.

AG   Less gun violence, better education, greater morality. So what you're basically saying, in the kind of simple language that even our leaders in Washington could understand, is that values education works.

DF   Yes, well, there seems to be evidence . . .

AG   That's great, Professor Fox, just great. Why do you think the liberal media doesn't want America to know about this?

DF   I'm not sure that the media is trying to suppress this. It's just that not many people have read my paper, and . . .

AG   Professor Fox, you're too modest. We hear from CROSS that you are one of the most influential young economists looking at social issues today.

DF   Uh . . .

AG   Professor Fox, what other types of values education should we see in America's schools?

DF   Alan, I'm not sure I can answer that, my paper is just about one teenage abstinence program.

AG   Don't you think, Professor Fox, that teaching intelligent design would go a long way toward instilling values in today's American youth?

DF   Intelligent design? You mean creationism?

AG   Whatever it's called, Professor Fox, it's the way to go, wouldn't you agree?

DF   I don't know, Alan, I think that the evidence for evolution . . .

AG   Great, thanks. We need to take a break and we'll be back in a minute with your calls. Do you want to ask Professor Fox a question about values education? Call us at 1-800-748-8255, that's 1-800-RIT-TALK.

[One-Minute Commercial Break]

AG   We're back. If you're just joining us, we're here with one of the most influential young economists in America today, Professor David Fox. Professor Fox has done pathbreaking work showing that values need to be taught in our public schools to stop the slide of morality that America is suffering today. Let's go to the calls. We have Curt from Kansas on the line.

CALLER 1   Alan, thanks for taking my call. As usual, a great show.

AG   Thanks, Curt, what's your question for Professor Fox?

CALLER 1: Professor Fox, is it true that Europeans don't share our values?

DF   Curt, I think people in Europe more or less share the same values that we do.

AG   But we all know, Professor Fox, that divorce rates in Europe are much higher than in the United States, and that there are many more out-of-wedlock births.

DF   I'm not sure about that, Alan.

AG   Believe me, you can look it up. Our next caller is Diane from New Hampshire. Got much snow up there in New Hampshire, Diane?

CALLER 2   Sure do, Alan. But we know how to handle it.

AG   I bet you do. What do you want to ask the professor today, Diane?

CALLER 2   Professor, how can I keep my daughters away from the trash that they show on TV?

DF   I guess you could just limit the hours they watch.

CALLER 2   Professor, do you have any daughters? Have you ever tried to pry kids away from TV?

AG   Diane, Professor Fox is a young scholar, devoted to his research. You don't have kids, do you, professor?

DF   No, Alan, I'm not even married.

AG   Hear that ladies, an eligible brilliant professor who's concerned about the moral climate in this country. You might want to get your daughters to apply to Kester College.

DF   Uh, Alan, I'm not sure that . . .

AG   We have time for one more call. Let's talk to Ron from Wisconsin. Ron, you're on the air.

CALLER 3   Hi. I'm a graduate student in economics at the University of Wisconsin. Professor Fox, can you explain why your research shows that teenage abstinence programs work while all the other research on this topic . . .

AG   Sorry, Ron, that's all we have time for in this segment. Professor David Fox of Kester College, thanks so much for speaking with America on *Talk Right*. We look forward to hearing a lot more about your important work.

DF   Thanks, Alan. Thanks a lot for this opportunity.

Chapter 19

And just like that, it was over.

Alan Glidden thanked him quickly once they went to commercial break, and then hung up. After a few seconds, David hung up too.

He looked at the digital clock on his desk. 5:25. If everyone got fifteen minutes of fame, he still had five minutes left. But he really didn't want it.

He looked out the window. It was dark.

He couldn't call anybody. No one he knew listened to *Talk Right*, and he didn't think he wanted anyone to know he was on the show.

Maybe Curt, Diane, and Ron were the only ones who listened. Why would Ron listen? Didn't he have anything better to do with his time in Madison than patrol the airwaves for right-wing nuts? Why wasn't he working on his dissertation? Why did he have to call in? What was he trying to prove?

A swim would be good. Or maybe a drink. Or maybe a swim and then a drink. But the Weissmuller Pool didn't open for free swim until 7:30.

A drink first, and then go swimming. No, bad idea. He could see if Angie wanted to get a drink and then go swimming. No, she was in Rochester today for work and wouldn't get back until Wednesday.

He stared out the window again. He would get something to eat. At home. And then go swimming. And then have a beer. Or two.

Probably no one listened to the show. At least no one he knew, or would ever meet.

David showed his ID to the student at the desk in the entrance hall of the Weissmuller Pool.

"Heard you on the radio today, Professor."

"What?"

"I heard you on *Talk Right*. Pretty cool."

"You listen to *Talk Right*?"

"Sure, it's fun. But I never heard anyone I knew interviewed on it before."

"Uh, thanks. Got to go swim now. See ya," he mumbled as he stuffed his ID back in his wallet and quickly turned to go to the locker room.

There were a few students in the locker room, in various stages of undress. One of them was Zach Rogowski from his Principles class, who greeted him enthusiastically.

"Professor Fox, you were awesome on the Glidden show."

"Thanks, Zach, thanks very much."

"Your research sounds really interesting. You should talk about that stuff in class."

"Maybe next semester. It's still kind of preliminary."

"Whatever. Anyway, it was great to hear one of my professors on a national radio show. See you around."

"Bye, Zach, see you later."

He turned to the locker, avoiding the glances of the others in the room who, all of a sudden, took an interest in the celebrity in their midst. He fiddled around with his combination lock for a while and then, sitting on the bench, took his time removing his boots and socks. Finally, everyone else left and he was alone in the locker room. He took advantage of the moment of solitude and quickly finished changing into his swimsuit.

That evening, David swam 2,500 yards, the most he had ever swum at one time in the Weissmuller Pool. He particularly liked the fact that, as he swam, all he could hear was the water splashing as his hands entered and left the water, and the sound of his own breath as he exhaled underwater and took in a breath when he turned his head to the side.

After stopping off to buy a six-pack, David walked back to his apartment. The new snow, still untainted by vehicle exhaust, traction sand, or the stains of dogs, reflected the lights from the streetlamps and muffled the sounds of the evening. The sky was clear, the stars were out, and it was cold. His arms and chest were tired from his swim, but tired in a way that felt good. He was looking forward to a beer when he got back to his apartment.

He entered his apartment, hung up his coat, and took off his boots. He walked into the darkened kitchen and, as he took one of the beers from the six-pack, saw the light on his phone message machine blinking. There were four new messages. He pushed the button.

"David, it's Mom. Sylvie Roth told me that she heard you on the radio today. Why didn't you tell us you were going to be on? Sylvie said you were talking about Kentucky and creationism. Does this have anything to do with that group you were telling us about on Thanksgiving? Call us back."

The machine beeped as it went to the next message. This time his father's voice came on.

"David, I know Mom just called you, but she hung up before I could get on the phone. What's this about you being on the radio? Was it *All Things Considered*? Call us up."

The machine beeped again. David heard the voice of his zaydie.

"Davie, your Mom just called and told me that you were on the national news. Mazel tov! Was this about your work? What TV station was it? Give me a call. Love you."

The machine beeped one more time, and, this time, he heard Angie's voice.

"Hi, David, just checking in. I guess you must be at the pool. Wish I was with you. Rochester got a lot of snow, more than we have in Knittersville. I'll be back on Wednesday. Good luck getting your applications out. Maybe now that you're a radio star you'll get more attention." At this point, the recorded message caught Angie's laugh for three or four seconds before she hung up.

David decided it was too late to return any of these phone calls tonight. After all, who is still up at 9:00 p.m. on a weekday? No, the responsible and proper thing to do would be to have a couple of these beers and then call it a night.

Chapter 20

Greg Shankle did not make a habit of listening to *Talk Right* on a regular basis, but he did try to tune in when he knew there would be a segment about economics. In fact, he liked to listen to any talk radio shows that discussed economics, even if the show typically had a liberal bias, like those broadcast on National Public Radio. Greg did not share these eclectic tastes with his friends in SAVE since, as far as he knew, most of them thought it inappropriate to waste time with the liberal media (his classmates claimed NPR stood for National Pinko Radio). But he had a different view of what was appropriate, based on an experience with his grandfather when he was much younger.

Greg's dad always told him that the bookworm trait skipped a generation. Greg and his grandpa shared a love of reading, and so, ever since he was young, a family visit to his grandparents typically involved the two of them going to the local library. On one of these visits, when Greg was in high school, he and his grandpa had agreed to meet in the periodical room at 3:00. When he got there, he found his grandfather at a table reading a plain paper magazine that he had never seen before.

"What's that magazine, Grandpa?"

"It's called the *Nation*, Greg."

"What's it about?"

"It's not about anything in particular. It has articles on lots of current events. It's pretty left-wing. I like to look at it when I get a chance."

Greg was shocked.

"Grandpa, what are you doing reading a left-wing magazine?"

"Greg," his grandfather replied, "it's natural to want to read something you agree with, but it's more important to make yourself read something you don't agree with."

Greg, and everyone else associated with CROSS, crowded into Bill Crocker's office at a little after 5:00 p.m. on Monday to listen to Alan Glidden interview David Fox on *Talk Right*. Extra chairs had been brought in to accommodate the staff. Bill Crocker sat behind his desk. As the show began, he leaned back in his swivel desk chair, his arms crossed over his chest, and turned his eyes toward the ceiling. His secretary, Pamela Winship, a very attractive woman that Greg was a little scared of, sat in the chair across the desk from Dr. Crocker. Some of the other staff sat on the couch. Greg had started off on the couch between two elderly women who helped with CROSS's direct mailing, but then moved to a metal folding chair that had been brought into the office to give up his seat for a third older woman whose job at CROSS, as far as he could tell, involved procuring donuts and making copies.

Everyone in Dr. Crocker's office cheered when Glidden mentioned CROSS in his introduction. As Fox answered Glidden's questions, and as Glidden himself gave them a spin that made them more accessible to his listeners, the three women on the couch played the role of the choir with their comments of "That's right," and "You tell them, now." At the commercial break, Dr. Crocker asked no one in particular, "This is going fine, isn't it?" In a pattern that Greg had noted was quite common, Pamela interpreted what many might have thought of as a rhetorical comment as a direct inquiry to her, and therefore answered, "Yes it is, Dr. Crocker, it's going very well." The three couch women backed up Pamela's assessment with "Yes it is," "Really fine," and "He's doing a real good job."

After the segment ended, Dr. Crocker stood up and addressed the room. "You can all be very proud of the fine work this organization is doing. The kind of national attention that we got this evening is just the beginning. It's because of all of you that we are where we are, and also it's because of you that we are going where we are going. Have a good evening, all, and see you tomorrow." The people in the office spontaneously applauded.

Greg and the others filed out of Dr. Crocker's office. All of the other people got their coats and left for the parking lot. Greg stayed behind since he had things he wanted to do. He had not completed any of the work he had brought home with him over the Thanksgiving holiday. In particular, he had fallen behind in his efforts to check the accuracy of Professor Fox's results, though he had made a fair amount of progress earlier that day. By his reckoning, it would only take another hour or so to complete his replications. He could then go on to his homework problem sets that were due at the end of the week.

As Greg started to look again at the programs sent to him by Professor Fox, he couldn't help but fantasize about a time when he, too, would be interviewed on national radio about his own economic research. Of course, he would need to first produce some economic research, and it would have to be as pathbreaking as Professor Fox's work in order to get any attention, but, still, it was good to have dreams and goals. He dreamed of being a professor, maybe even at SAVE, and he knew that his goal of finishing a quality PhD was one way that dream could be realized. He thought he would be a good teacher. He would share with his students both his understanding of economics and his vision of how its analytical tools could be used to improve the world.

Greg tried not to lose sight of the importance of using the tools of economics for moral ends, but he also liked the tools themselves and found using them very satisfying. As far as he could tell, other disciplines could make some suggestions about why things happened the way they did, or what caused people to act in certain ways but, with economics and its statistical tools, you could darn near *prove*, with statistical certainty, why things turned out as they did. If only faith was certain, well, at least economic results were near certain.

He had only two more of Fox's computer programs to check, line by line, and then he could rerun the results. He brought up the first of these programs and began to scroll down, following the code and tracing out, in his mind, its logical sequence. All seemed correct until he got about two-thirds of the way through the program. One of Fox's commands, as far as he could tell, caused the data to be incorrectly resampled. He doubted that this was really a mistake; it was probably his own error in thinking through the logic of the code. He started diagramming the command structure on a pad of paper. After checking twice, and coming up with the same conclusion each time, he realized that Fox had made a small error in the coding by writing $i = 1, n$ when he should have written $j = 1, n$. It was easy enough to fix. He then checked through the last, relatively short, program, and it seemed correct.

Greg was getting tired, but he was near the end of this task for CROSS and he wanted to complete it and move on to his own homework. All that was left for him to do was to use the data sent to him by Fox to replicate the results. He would run the series of five programs, including the one in which he had made the minor correction, and then compare his results to the ones in the *CROSS Currents* working paper that had inspired so much discussion on national radio earlier that evening. He ran each of the programs in turn. When the fifth and final program was completed, he looked at the output on the screen to see how these results compared with the ones in Fox's paper.

Greg did not need to look at Fox's paper to know that the results he saw in glowing green numbers on his computer screen did not match those in black and white in the working paper on his desk. This wasn't a question of being off by a few tenths of a percent; the results on his computer completely differed from what Fox had published. According to what he was looking at, teenage abstinence programs actually *increased* pregnancy rates! Scrolling down, he found that his new results provided no evidence that the abstinence programs affected the number of instances of gun confiscation, or of the grades on standardized tests. These new results suggested that the "Something for Nothing" should be given the new, much less felicitous title "Nothing for Nothing, or Even Worse."

He felt an emptiness in his stomach that wasn't related to the fact that he had not yet had dinner. He reran each of the five programs again and carefully checked the results at each stage against those sent to him by Fox. His results lined up with those of Fox for the first program, and for the second, and for the third. But the correction in the fourth program, a change that had seemed relatively minor, altered its results dramatically from those that Fox had obtained. The use of these corrected results in the fifth program changed the final estimates in a way that completely altered the message of the paper. Though he was sure that the mistake was an honest one, and Professor Fox had just made a simple programming error, the fact was that Crocker, CROSS, Alan Glidden, the nation's *Talk Right* Rebels, Greg, and even Fox himself had been misled.

Subject: In your midst
Date: 11/26/2007, 8:22 PM
To: Randolph Carlson <randolph.carlson@kester.edu>
From: Leo Miles <antiglobalguy@gmail.com>

Hey, Randy,

Monitoring the airwaves tonight, I heard a colleague of yours interviewed by that asshole Glidden. Guy's name is Fox, teaches economics (it figures, right?). Sounds like a right-wing jerk. What kind of teachers you got up there? Hope you can set him straight.

Later,
Leo

"Our objective is complete freedom, justice and equality *by any means necessary.*"
—Malcolm X

Chapter 21

Randolph Carlson, like all the other professors at Kester College, had done the post-Thanksgiving calculation on material remaining to be covered versus time available. But, unlike the other professors who also spent September, October, and early November regaling their students with political opinions, personal reflections, and witty asides, Randy (as he requested the students call him) found that he had too little, rather than too much, material for his final five lectures in his course Threats to Liberty. It wasn't that there were too few instances in the world of the extreme right oppressing freedom of thought and action; it was just that he didn't spend enough time preparing lectures.

Randolph had faced this problem before. Before he had tenure, he had been deeply concerned about student evaluations, and scrambled during the last weeks of the semester to come up with new material. He was able to face this end-of-semester quandary with more equanimity once the threat of being denied tenure passed. Also, better student evaluations would not get him promoted to full professor, and, even if they did, the promotion came with an insignificant increase in pay. Thus, lacking incentives to be better prepared for his class, he found himself improvising in late November and early December. Last year, he had spent two classes discussing how corporate America was co-opting the organic food movement in its efforts to head off the real threat of a people's uprising against genetically modified foods. At one point, he dramatically took a bag of Doritos out of the hands of a student and riffed on corporate manipulation of the 18–24-year-old demographic. This was good for twenty-five minutes of class time. Two years ago, on a particularly cold day, Randolph spent almost the entire class period recounting how, when he was a student, the members of the communal house where he lived decided to protest the reliance of the United States on nonrenewable energy sources by keeping their thermostat at 58 degrees for the entire winter. He did not mention, however, how his electric blanket helped him weather this period of hardship.

On the Monday evening after Thanksgiving break, Randolph was at his desk at home, surfing the web and looking for some good examples of injustice that he could talk about in class the next day. Then he received an e-mail from his old comrade-in-arms, Leo Miles. Randolph shared Miles's views about a good many things, but he also thought that Miles was a few aces short of a full deck. After all, what kind of guy would spend an hour or two each day monitoring right-wing talk radio? Not that he would ever say this to Miles, or to any of the people they knew in common, since, for the cause, it was probably important that Miles, or people like him, kept tabs on what the other side was doing. But still—come on, guy—get a life.

Tonight, however, Randolph was actually glad to receive Miles's message. This was just the type of thing that he could use to fill up two, or even three, of the remaining five lectures in his course. A month or two ago, Fox made some wise-ass comment to him in the cafeteria. That other economist, White, apologized for him, but it still rankled him that some young professor, one who was only a visitor for chrissakes, felt as if he could talk back to a tenured professor like that. Still, it might be a little dicey to attack another professor by name since some of the kids might know him and try to defend him. No, it would be better to be a bit more oblique and just talk about abstinence programs. Enough of the kids would know who he was speaking about to get the full meaning of his message. Besides, what college kid would be *for* abstinence?

"As you know, we have only five more meetings this semester. I'd love to carry on this conversation with you into late December, and even January, because there is so much that the right wing in this country is trying to do to stop you and the people from understanding how things are really going down. But, alas, even Threats to Liberty is not completely free, and we must bend to the will of the university and follow its calendar."

At this, Randolph surreptitiously looked at his watch. Having spent some time at the beginning of class asking students how their parents had reacted to what they had told them about this course during their Thanksgiving break, he now had one hour left in the class.

"Maybe the most important liberty of all is the liberty to use our bodies in the ways they were meant to be used. Freedom of expression is not just in the written word, or in spoken conversation, but in physical acts as well."

At this, Randolph paused for a second and redirected his view from the top of the back wall to the students sitting in front of him. They were writing it all down, as they always did. This next part was going to be fun.

"Sex," he said, and then paused for dramatic effect. It worked. Everyone stopped writing and looked at him.

"Yes, you heard me right, sex. After all, what physical act is more human than the act of love, either between a man and a woman, or a man and a man, or a woman and a woman, or among a group of people bound together by a common belief?"

That got their attention. A few of the students would have giggled, had it not been so uncool to do so. This was serious, this was liberty, this wasn't some version of *American Pie*.

"There are many ways in which the right wing wants to stop sex. Of course, there are sodomy laws in many states. But it goes beyond that. Well beyond that. The newest conspiracy is abstinence programs. The government wants to enforce behavior that goes against human nature. If the government can stop sex, then it can also stop any other effort by people to organize politically in an effort to realize their own liberty."

Randolph liked the way he was spinning this, how he had linked sex, which all of the students would want (even if only a subset of them regularly got it), to political liberties, which seemed pretty abstract to nineteen-year-olds from privileged backgrounds. Isn't this the way teaching values was meant to be, to make the personal political?

"Randy, if the government is so against sex, how come they allow so much of it to be shown on TV?" asked Frieda, a girl in the class that he had watched with interest throughout the semester.

"Frieda, that's a really good point. By allowing sex to be shown on TV shows, and in movies, the government is objectifying it in a way that allows corporations to profit. At the same time, however, the government can control the way in which sex is portrayed and remove from the portrayal any political element." ("Oh, you're good Randolph," he thought.)

"Randy, why doesn't everyone realize this?" asked Ben the Earnest, the name he secretly gave to the sophomore who had already taken two of his classes.

"Ben, as you know from the other work we have done in this class and the one you took with me last spring, the people who work on this are very clever. It takes a high level of analysis to see through the smokescreen they create."

"You know, Professor Fox was on the radio last night talking about abstinence programs," added Melanie. ("Bingo," Randolph thought.)

"I didn't know that," said Randolph. "What did he say?"

Melanie, a tall, attractive junior who he hoped would write a senior thesis with him next year, said, "He did some research on how abstinence programs had all these good effects. It was on one of those right-wing talk shows. It was pretty gross, actually."

"Now, now, Melanie, I'm sure Professor Fox thought his work was doing good in the world. It's sad, though, how scientists, or people who think what they do is *social science*, can't see how their supposedly 'neutral' work can have tremendously destructive effects. It's like Oppenheimer, and the others who worked on the Manhattan project."

Given their blank stares, he realized that he had to explain the Manhattan project, and the use of science for weapons. This, of course, was a very rich vein, and one that easily took him to the end of the time allotted to class that day.

As the students filed out, chatting among themselves, Randolph thought, "Now only four classes left."

Chapter 22

On the last day of classes of the fall semester, David was in his office early in the morning to look over the final PowerPoint slides for his courses. He had placed the full set of PowerPoint slides for his Principles of Economics course in one neat stack on his desk, and the full set of slides for his Economics of Social Issues course in another stack. These two stacks represented most of his productivity during the fall. He felt good about the courses that he taught, thinking that the students who had applied themselves and followed the material had really learned some useful concepts and tools. This feeling of pride, however, was mixed with one of anxiety. No matter how good a teacher he proved to be, the coin of the realm, as Minard had told him at the beginning of the semester, was publications. There was no third stack on his desk representing his research output during the fall. He had managed to massage one dissertation chapter enough to send it out with his applications, but it was not in good enough shape yet for it to be submitted to a scholarly journal. There was "Something for Nothing," but his work for that during this semester had really involved nothing more than getting a *CROSS Currents* title page placed on top of the paper he wrote three years ago.

Just after 9:40, David's phone rang.

"Hello?"

"Professor David Fox?" a woman's voice asked.

"Yes, this is Professor Fox."

"Professor Fox, this is Professor Linda Goldman. I'm the chair of the hiring committee at Brunsfield College."

His heart began to beat faster.

"Oh, hi, good morning."

"Professor Fox, we were hoping to have the chance to interview you at the American Economics Association convention in Boston. Do you have any time slots available on January 3 or 4?"

"I think I have some availability during those days," he answered, attempting to not sound too anxious.

"Great. We were concerned that, with all this notoriety you've been enjoying, we might be too late in trying to get an interview with you."

He wondered, for a minute, about what Goldman meant by "notoriety," but then realized that she may have been responding to the *USA Today* clipping he had included with his application. He hoped Goldman wasn't a regular listener of *Talk Right*.

"No, I still have some time slots left. What time were you thinking of?"

"How about 11:00 on January 4? We will have a suite at the Marriott."

"Let me look at my schedule." He paused for, what he hoped, was a credible amount of time. "Yes, 11:00 should work."

"That's wonderful," said Professor Goldman with what sounded like real enthusiasm in her voice. "We're looking forward to meeting you. We'll send you some information, and, of course, you can check out our department online. We think you'll find that, even though we are a traditional liberal arts college, there's a really good research environment here."

"That sounds great." He had no difficulty at all in conveying the enthusiasm he felt.

"Good. Again, if there's anything I can do to let you know more about Brunsfield, please don't hesitate to contact me."

"Thanks, thanks very much."

"We'll be in touch. Have a good morning."

"Thank you, Professor Goldman. You, too."

David hung up the phone, and then punched both fists in the air.

He sat at his desk, thinking about his good fortune. He decided to share his good news with Angie. But, just before he picked up the phone, he heard a knock at his door.

"Come in."

Murray Stern entered his office, carrying a newspaper. He liked Murray, and chatted with him when they saw each other in the halls. They also occasionally had meals together, though these lunches occurred when they ran into each other in the cafeteria rather than because of prior planning. But this was Murray's first time visiting him in his office.

"Hi, Murray. Happy end of semester."

"And to you, David. And congratulations on your newfound fame."

"What?"

Murray unfolded the newspaper he was carrying, which turned out to be the *Wall Street Journal*. He opened the paper to the op-ed page and pointed to the third editorial, entitled "Education Programs That Work." David began to read the editorial, which seemed to be about states' efforts to be innovative in providing high school education. He stopped and stared when he came to the clause "as shown by Professor David Fox of Kester College, in a working paper published by the Center to Research Opportunities for a Spiritual Society (CROSS)."

167

"Murray, what is this?"

"That paper we talked about way back in September is getting a lot of attention. I heard you were interviewed on a national radio show."

"Murray, I'd just as soon forget about that."

"David, it's not very common for an economist at a place like Kester to get this kind of attention. You should be glad. As much as we like to think that universities are pure meritocracies, a lot of professors get ahead by getting known."

David made a connection. "I just got a call this morning for an interview at the AEA meetings. The person who called said something about my notoriety. I didn't know what she was talking about, but it must be this *Wall Street Journal* editorial."

"That's really great. I'm very glad for you." He paused for a moment. "You know that we're hiring this year, too. I've heard some good things about your classes. I know that you've given us an application, and we'll be considering you for a position. I hope that you haven't thought that we weren't interested in you. We just had our meeting a couple of days ago, and we have been busy phoning people to set up initial interviews. We don't feel we need to interview you at the AEA meetings since we know you already. But we hope that we can consider you a part of our second-round applicant pool. If nothing else, we can save money on airfare for your fly-out."

If David had not already had a call from Brunsfield, and if he had not seen the *Wall Street Journal* editorial, he might have been concerned about the amount of truth behind Murray's joke that he only got to the second round because of the money Kester would save on airfare. But, given this new information, he was able to join in Murray's laughter at his last comment.

David thought a lot about how he would end his last class of his first semester of teaching. As an undergraduate, he had joined in enthusiastic applause when many of his classes concluded. In most of those cases, he actually felt a sense of appreciation toward the professor for putting together an interesting course. He knew that an applause-o-meter was a poor indicator of how much students enjoyed a class, and even less of an indicator of how much they had learned. Nevertheless, given how little positive reinforcement new professors enjoyed, he fantasized about a standing ovation that confirmed his accomplishments during the fall.

He had asked Jeff White a week ago how students responded at the conclusion of a course. Jeff told him that, for the most part, students gave a smattering of polite applause. There were cases of tremendously enthusiastic applause, though not in economics courses. Some courses even ended without any recognition, with students closing their notebooks and silently filing out of the room.

"That must be so disappointing."

"The thing is, you have to work for it," Jeff explained. "If you end your final class with something like 'And thus, we can show that demand curves slope downward,' there isn't much of a buildup, is there? You have to end with drama and an appeal to emotions. Something more like"—Jeff's voice deepened, and his enunciation became more pronounced—"And so we see that all material human progress, indeed all human endeavor, can be explained with demand and supply. Thus, I leave you today a wiser, kinder, and more generous class than I found you in September. Go forth, my students, go forth and show the world what we here at Kester can do." With that, Jeff took a theatric bow.

"You don't really do that, do you?"

"Not quite all of it. But I do try a little bit of a buildup, so at least they remember that it's the last day of classes."

David thought of this conversation as he walked to the final class meeting of his Economics of Social Issues. But, during the class, caught up with covering the material he had left, he forgot about building up to a grand conclusion. Instead, with only one minute left in the period, he finished discussing the last Power-Point slide.

"Okay, so that's it," he concluded. "I hope you liked the class this semester. I had fun teaching it. I also hope you felt you learned something. I guess the main thing I wanted you to learn was not so much a set of facts, but a way of thinking about issues. What I really like about economics is that you can use it to think for yourself about things that are pretty important in people's lives. I hope that this class helped you see that."

As soon as he finished this sentence spoken to Jenny, Brooke, Julia, Stephen, Jay, Melissa, Charlotte, Akshay, Maureen, and fifteen other students whose names he had learned, he felt a little deflated, thinking that his words had failed to fully convey his feelings. The enthusiastic applause of the twenty-four students in the class, however, showed that his students, once more, understood him well.

Chapter 23

There are lots of wonderful things about being a professor, but grading is not one of them. Students need to be evaluated, but can you really tell how much someone knows from a few exams, or a couple of papers? And how do you know an evaluation has not been colored by factors other than academic performance? It's easy to impute a depth of knowledge that may not really be there when a student is particularly earnest, or hardworking, or, let's be truthful now, good-looking.

These concerns went through David's mind as he sat at the desk in his office, slowly working his way through the stack of exam books from his Principles of Economics course. These students, many of them in their first semester, would judge themselves and their future prospects partly by the grade they got in this class. He might be changing lives here. If he was too stingy in grading a couple of questions, a student may get a B+ instead of an A- and, as a result, decide against majoring in economics. But if he was too lenient, a student may go down a path for which she had no natural aptitude, only to be crushed later on. This was a weighty task.

It was also a colossal pain in the ass, and tremendously boring. David had two stacks of exam books on his desk, a short stack with exams that he had finished grading and a much taller stack with exams that he had not yet evaluated. After an hour of work, it seemed that the tall stack grew no shorter while the short stack stayed stubbornly diminutive. David knew he was making progress since he kept counting the number of exam books in each stack. But this mathematical certainty did nothing to alter his subjective view that there was no change in the relative heights of the two stacks.

Frequent interruptions contributed to the apparent slow progress in completing the task at hand. Most of these interruptions were self-inflicted. For example, cups of tea helped make grading more palatable, and the only way to get a cup was to go to the faculty lounge and wait for the water to boil in the English-style electric kettle there. The kettle was a gift to the department from its chairman. Therefore, it would have been rude of David not to engage Professor Wellingham in conversation when he wandered into the faculty lounge while the water was heating up. There was, of course, also a strategic motive to chat with Professor Wellingham since he would likely have a big role in the upcoming hiring decision. Thus, it would have been shortsighted of him to interrupt the discursive explanation of the origins of Boxing Day just so he could get back to his office to grade exams. But, once he did get back to his office, all those cups of tea slowed him down once again as he kept getting up to go to the men's room at the other end of the hall.

After a period during which an outside observer would have concluded that Professor Fox suffered from attention deficit disorder, David decided to think about grading the way he thought about swimming laps. It would have been very difficult to get into the pool and, during your first lap, think about how there were fifty-nine more laps to go. It was much easier to tell yourself a little fib; once I complete the first 200 yards, I can decide whether or not to swim another 200 yards. After the second 200, there was always the option of not starting on the third 200. Of course, this was a lie. There was no way he would stop swimming after 200 yards, or after 400, or after anything short of at least 1,500. But breaking up an imposing goal into a series of smaller, more manageable tasks made the whole process less daunting.

Employing this strategy of self-deception ("I only need to grade these two exams, and then I can stop"), David made much better progress. After another two hours, the completed stack was taller than the stack of exams waiting to be graded. David thought that he might finish all the grading for this course by the end of the day. That would just leave the papers and exams for the Economics of Social Issues class to be graded.

A knock on his office door broke his concentration.

"Come in," he said, with a little more impatience than he had intended.

Jenny Lake opened the door but did not enter. "If this is a bad time, I could come back later."

It was a bad time, but it was always nice to see Jenny. "No, it's fine. Come on in. Have a seat."

Jenny entered the office and closed the door behind her. She took off her parka and held it in her lap as she sat across from David.

"I just wanted to say thanks for all the time you spent working with me this semester. I really appreciate it. I learned a lot, and I'll be working on my thesis over the break. Hopefully, I'll make some progress."

"It was nice working with you, Jenny. You've already made a lot of progress. I think your thesis will turn out well."

"Do you really think so?"

"Yeah, I do. You have a great data set from the town, and you've crafted a good question, one that you can answer with the data you have. It'll still take some work, of course, but you're on the right path."

"That's so nice of you to say. It's been really fun working with you."

"It's been fun working with you, too."

"I got you a present, I guess it would be a Chanukah present, but really it's just to thank you for all the time you spent with me this fall."

Jenny smiled, reached into the pocket of her coat, and pulled out a small brightly wrapped package.

David's pleasure at having his efforts recognized was tempered by a concern about whether it was appropriate to accept a gift from a student whose work he had yet to grade. But looking at her pretty, earnest face, he couldn't imagine that she meant to influence his decision with this small gesture of gratitude. And besides, she didn't have to try to influence him, she was smart enough to get really good grades anyway.

"Jenny, thank you very much. This is totally unnecessary, but it's sweet of you to do this." His hand brushed hers as he took the small package from her. It was surprisingly heavy for something so small.

"Open it."

He smiled as he unwrapped the paper. It was a shot glass, with the Kester College crest inscribed on it and, under that, the college's motto "Integritas."

"That's so thoughtful. Thanks very much."

"You're welcome. I thought you should have something with Kester on it."

"Thanks."

"I was also thinking that maybe sometime we could use it together, and get a drink or something."

He looked up from the shot glass to see Jenny looking at him intently. She was smiling, but not as broadly as a moment ago and her green eyes had become a little more hooded. He didn't know what to say. He didn't know what he wanted to say.

"Oh, well, that would be nice. We'll have to find a time, maybe when you turn in your thesis."

"That would be great. Maybe even before that." She stood up and spread her arms. "Happy New Year, Professor Fox."

He stood up, too, and gave her a hug. It would have been rude to have left her standing there, especially after she was nice enough to give him this gift. As with their first hug, it felt like her breasts were leaving an imprint on his chest. And, since this hug lasted longer, he also felt an imprint from the rest of her as well. He then caught himself, and broke the hug. "Happy holidays to you too, Jenny."

"I hope the new year holds good things in store for you, Professor Fox."

"I hope we all get what we want in the new year, Jenny," he said, and, he thought, "whatever that is."

Chapter 24

"So I arranged the interviews from Thursday through Saturday in a way that none of them are back-to-back. It wasn't easy, since I have fourteen, not counting Kester of course, but it seemed really important to try to schedule them so I wouldn't have to rush from one to the next."

David and Angie were dining at the Cask and Barrel. They had not seen each other for a week, since Angie had been traveling for work. David kept busy grading exams during that time. He had also spent the week fielding calls from the chairs of hiring committees, many of whom referred to the *Wall Street Journal* editorial that mentioned his work. The phone calls slowed his grading, but he certainly didn't mind. He was more concerned with another impediment to grading, replaying Jenny Lake's last visit to his office in his mind over and over again. He hadn't done anything inappropriate, and you can't be prosecuted for the thoughts running through your head. But the whole incident still bothered him, or at least it left him hot and bothered.

This dinner had been planned before Angie left town. They figured the evening would be a celebration of the end of David's first semester at Kester. The past week was more eventful than he had expected, however, and he just finished grading the last of the papers for the Social Issues course (Jenny received an A, legitimately). He rushed through grading the last two papers, but he was still fifteen minutes late for dinner.

"You never told me how your students did."

"Oh, right. They did pretty well. There's always a distribution of the grades. A couple of kids in Principles did very well; they got in the high nineties."

"That must be gratifying. You really taught them something. How about your other course? How were the papers?"

"Pretty good."

"Any As?"

"A couple. The students who got As really deserved them."

"I'm sure they did. I bet the students love you."

"What do you mean by that?"

Angie looked at him for a moment. "Nothing. Just that you must feel good about your teaching."

"Yeah, it's nice." He brightened, saying, "The good thing is, I can talk about my teaching experience, and especially my Social Issues course, in my interviews. It's a real advantage to have already taught my own course. Most of the people coming directly out of a PhD program won't have that experience."

Angie paused before speaking again. "I was thinking, I might be able to arrange to meet with one of my clients near Boston on the Thursday you're at the meetings. We could stay together in Boston on Friday, and maybe on Saturday night we could go to a play or something."

"That's probably not a good idea." But as soon as these words were out of his mouth, he regretted it.

"Why not?" Angie said, her voice rising. "Are you planning to be there with someone else?"

"No, Angie, of course not."

"Well, are you afraid of being seen with your girlfriend from the boonies when you're in Boston?"

"No, Angie. Look, it's not that at all. It's just that I have all these interviews and I'm going to be really distracted."

"Yeah, I know about your interviews, and I certainly know about you being distracted. You called me only once all last week when I was away. And the only thing that you talked about the week before that was your interviews."

"I thought you would be happy for me."

"I am happy for you, I'm really happy, but c'mon David, can we talk about something other than your job for once?"

"That's not fair. We talk about other stuff all the time."

"Yeah? What else have we talked about recently? Have you asked me anything about my job, or my plans for the holidays? Have you even made any plans to spend any part of the holidays with me?"

He realized that he had not even thought about buying a Christmas present for her. But couldn't she see that this was a turning point for him?

"Look, Angie, this is my career. This is a big deal for me."

"I know, but it seems like I'm not that big a deal for you anymore."

"Angie . . . ," he began.

"What?" she demanded. "You've becoming totally wrapped up in yourself and your job search. You can't see anything else." She paused and looked him directly in the eyes. "You've become really boring," she declared.

He stared at Angie. How dare she! This was his life. Jenny Lake was glad for him. Then he caught himself. What was he thinking? This is Angie, not some twenty-two-year-old coed. This is someone he truly cared for. What did she mean? Did she mean that he *was* boring, or that he had been acting in a boring way recently? He searched her face for some clarification, a face that he thought he knew how to read, but at this moment it was a mask hiding what he desperately wanted to know.

"Well, okay, what do you want to talk about?" There was a little more edge to his voice than he intended.

"Just forget it." She stared at her plate and focused on her entrée. He looked at the top of her head. Her dark, thick hair caught the low light from the candle on the table. He thought about how it felt to run his hands through her hair.

They sat like this for a few minutes, David attempting to will Angie to look up at him and Angie pushing the food around on her plate, occasionally lifting her fork to take a small bite. Finally, he broke the silence, saying in a soft voice, "Angie, I'm sorry. Maybe you should come to Boston."

When Angie looked up, he saw that she had tears in her eyes.

"David, I'm not sure this is such a good idea."

"You mean coming to Boston?"

"No, I mean us."

He stared at her. Where had this come from? Everything had been going well with them, at least until they got onto this last discussion. Maybe he did forget to call her last week, but he was busy. Couldn't she understand that? And why wasn't she happy that he got all these interviews, more than twice as many as last year?

This changed everything. He was getting to like Kester. He was even getting to like Knittersville a little. But he liked the Knittersville he shared with Angie, the Knittersville where he and Angie swam together, the Knittersville where he and Angie went out to eat, or where they stayed in at his apartment and then spent the night together. He had a sudden image of himself alone in his apartment, alone in the evenings, alone on long Sunday afternoons. His chest felt empty.

"Angie, we've been having a good time together, haven't we?"

Angie sighed, and answered in a softer voice than the one she had been using. "Look, it's had its moments, but I keep feeling that for some time now it's been all about you. It's not just the last couple of weeks, with the interviews. You haven't really showed much interest in me or my life for a while."

"I care about you, I ask you about . . ."

"Maybe we should just take some time off. You're going to be really busy with these interviews, and I've got a lot of family obligations for the holidays. How about we check back in sometime after the new year?"

He seemed to get tunnel vision. Everything else in the restaurant disappeared as he stared at Angie. What did she mean about checking in after the new year? Should he be hopeful? Every relationship has its rocky moments, right? A little time off might not be a bad thing. Or was Angie giving him the permanent brush-off? Again, he tried to read her face for a deeper meaning to her words, but all he could see was the sadness in her eyes. He thought she looked especially beautiful. He thought his heart would break.

"Okay, Angie, after the new year."

New Year

Chapter 25

A–F; G–M; N–Z.

A–F.

"David Fox."

The woman seated behind the counter shuffled through the large envelopes in the box in front of her, and then selected one, drew it out, and handed it, along with a blue canvas bag, across the counter to him.

"Here you are Mr. Fox. Welcome to Boston."

He opened the envelope as he turned and walked away from the counter. He took out the paperback directory of sessions, the loose papers that included a hotel map, and his name tag ("DAVID" in large font, "Professor David Fox" below that in smaller font, and "Kester College" in somewhat smaller font on the third line) and placed them all in the bag that showed its owner was a participant in the "American Economic Association 2008 Annual Conference, Boston, Massachusetts." Normally, he would not flaunt this bag, or even use it in public, for fear of looking geeky. Here, however, he would be just one of thousands of others in a blue blazer, or a tweed coat, or (for the women) a sensible pantsuit, with a name tag and a blue canvas bag.

David looked at his watch once more and saw that he still had twenty minutes to walk over to Room 315 in the Westin Hotel for his first interview at 9:00. The decision to stay in town at a hotel for a couple of nights, rather than continue to stay at his parents' house where he had been since a couple of days after he turned in his final exams, was one of the better choices he had made lately. As he told his parents, commuting into Boston from the suburbs could be dicey, and he didn't want to put his career at the mercy of notoriously fickle Boston traffic; the job search process itself was already stressful enough. He did not mention to his parents an even more important reason for his decision to stay at a hotel for a couple of nights: the need to be free of their well-meaning, but seemingly unending, questions.

He felt a little guilty about this. As always, his parents were very pleased to host him, and, in this case, a little surprised as well. He had not spent this much time in "his room" since its bed had been replaced with a pullout couch more than five years ago. And his parents' questions were really not that unreasonable, or that unceasing. He just didn't want to have to explain again how the job process worked (cruelly and inefficiently), what his chances were (long at best), how he would try to present himself (modestly, but with some assurance), and which of the schools he had applied to he would prefer (any). His mother also sensed that there was more affecting his mood than just the job search but, demonstrating a discretion that he did not know she possessed, she asked him only once if anything else was bothering him and, receiving a vague answer, did not raise the question again.

In fact, his concerns flitted back and forth between anxiety about his interviews and anxiety about his relationship, if one still existed, with Angie. A few days after their last dinner together, he began to look forward to January, and the new year, when they had agreed to reconnect. But, as he replayed their final conversation over in his mind, he wasn't sure that the "new year" that Angie meant actually began on January 1. He was worried about calling Angie too soon after New Year's Day and, in so doing, demonstrating that he could follow directions but really had no clue. He was equally concerned about not calling her soon enough, which she might incorrectly interpret as a signal of his indifference.

So here it was, three days into the new year, and he had not yet attempted to call Angie. He thought he would give it a few more days. At first, in plotting this strategy, he thought he would wait until after all his interviews were completed. Then he could call Angie under the pretext of sharing some good news with her about his job search. But it took only a minute's reflection to realize that, given the topic of their last conversation, this probably wasn't a good idea. He also toyed with the idea of recanting, and inviting her to come stay with him at his hotel in Boston after the conference, but then he worried that would be asking for too much too soon. Finally, he decided to just try to focus on his interviews and, after those were completed, to go back to Knittersville and try to reconnect with her there.

The cold air that hit David as he walked the two blocks from the Marriott to the Westin took him out of this reverie about Angie and brought his mind back to the task at hand. He went over the names and positions of the people he was about to meet from Grindle College: Professor Mitchell Fredricks, chair of the search committee, who taught courses in macroeconomics, and Professor Lisa Trestin, a senior professor who taught labor economics. The Economics Department at Grindle had advertised for an assistant professor to teach Public Economics, and his experience in developing and teaching his course on The Economics of Social Issues must have attracted their attention. He guessed that the search committee had also been interested in him because the dissertation chapter that he had sent them concerned environmental economics, an area that falls within the broader category of public economics.

He arrived at the Westin at 8:50 and went to the bank of elevators. When he got there, he discovered a crowd of men and women about his age, all of whom were wearing suits with an AEA name tag on the lapel. An elevator door opened, and a group crowded in, leaving many more outside the elevator. One of those left in the lobby cried out, "I have a 9:00 appointment with Brandeis on the twenty-third floor." Heartbreaking as this was, there was no assurance that the Brandeis applicant, or anyone else, would win in the next round of elevator roulette. David quickly decided to opt out of this game of chance and walk up the two flights to Room 315.

He was only a little winded when he got to the third floor (all that swimming during the fall semester had paid off). He found Room 315 and knocked.

"Come in."

He entered the room and introduced himself. Professor Fredricks, a man of about sixty, wearing a tweed coat, introduced himself and Professor Trestin, a middle-aged woman in a sensible pantsuit. On a small table was a carafe of coffee and cups in saucers.

"Coffee?" Professor Fredricks asked.

"No, thank you." He had planned ahead of time to refuse all offers of food or drink during these interviews.

"It's a pleasure to get a chance to meet you, David—we can call you David, can't we?" Professor Fredricks asked.

"Sure, Professor Fredricks."

"Mitchell, please. David, you have a made an impressive start in your career, and we're very pleased that you've shown an interest in Grindle."

He was flattered but also a bit puzzled. He had not, to his mind, sprinted quickly out of the starting blocks. Some of his friends in graduate school had already had one or even two papers accepted for publication, and a couple were at top-ranked departments. But this was not the time to argue.

"Thanks very much."

Professor Trestin added, "We think that Grindle has a lot to offer someone like you."

He saw the opening and began his spiel. "I'm sure that I would like Grindle. As you can see from my CV, I've had wonderful opportunities at Kester to teach my own courses, and I really value the experience I've had in the classroom there. I've enjoyed introducing students to the powerful tools that economics teaches us. I also feel that I've made some good progress in getting chapters from my dissertation ready for submission. The articles from these chapters are on environmental economics, so you can see that I'm doing research in an area close to the position you're trying to fill."

"Yes, we looked at those papers," said Professor Trestin. "But we were wondering why you didn't include 'Something for Nothing' in your application packet."

"You're getting quite a reputation from that work," Professor Fredricks added.

David had hoped to avoid this discussion. Even though "Something for Nothing" had gotten him an invitation to the party, he wanted to ditch it now that he had arrived. But, like a bad date, it seemed as if his teenage abstinence paper was going to hang onto his arm and stay with him all evening.

"Thanks, but that paper was really a bit of a diversion for me. I see myself working more in the field of demand analysis with applications to environmental issues."

The expression on the interviewers' faces showed their disappointment.

"On the other hand," he quickly added, "questions of the impact of values education programs raise a lot of interesting points."

Professors Fredricks and Trestin leaned forward as he continued his riff on the econometric and theoretical issues related to an analysis of educational intervention programs. This was all improvisation on his part. He had scripted his discussion of his dissertation work, his teaching experience, and even his questions about Grindle, but he had not planned to talk about "Something for Nothing." The smoothness with which he launched into this discussion, however, surprised him. Later, reflecting on the ease with which he was able to extemporaneously expound on this topic, he realized that he must have been having some internal, ongoing dialogue about it ever since he got that first e-mail from CROSS.

It had become quite an animated discussion, and, after a while, Professor Trestin glanced at her watch and said, "Oh my, it looks like we only have a couple of minutes left. We should ask you, David, if you have any questions for us?"

"No, not really."

"In that case, I have one final question," Professor Fredricks said. "What is Alan Glidden really like?"

Chapter 26

A–F; G–M; N–Z.

N–Z.

"Greg Shankle."

"Could you spell that please?"

"S-H-A-N-K-L-E."

"Thank you, Mr. Shankle. Welcome to Boston."

Greg peered inside the envelope the woman behind the counter had handed to him. Inside was a guidebook listing the conference presentations, some loose papers, and a name tag (GREG/Greg Shankle/CROSS–SAVE).

"Mr. Shankle, you also get this bag," the woman said, as she handed him a blue canvas bag with "American Economic Association 2008 Annual Conference, Boston, Massachusetts" written on it. "Cool," he said to himself. He took his envelope and his bag to a chair at the side of the room and sat down.

The paperback book in the envelope had a list of all the research papers that would be presented in all the sessions that would be held over the next three days. He paged through the book for a few minutes. He noticed names of some Nobel laureates, as well as the names of people who, because of their contributions to the literature, were well known, at least to other economists. But, in a book that thick, most of the names were not ones that he, or any other economist, would know. He was a bit amazed at this evidence of so many economists doing so much work with so little recognition.

The fact that, at this convention, you could find so many economists doing so much work was exactly why he had made this trip. In early December, Pamela Winship, Dr. Crocker's secretary, had come to see him at his cubicle to tell him that Dr. Crocker would like to see him. Greg felt his heart race a bit, both because of the messenger and because of the possible message. Perhaps Dr. Crocker had also gone through the code of Professor Fox's program and had discovered the same mistake that he'd found. Dr. Crocker would be well within his rights to fire Greg for not alerting him to this problem, one that could fatally splinter CROSS.

The truth was that he was scared to let Dr. Crocker know that the "Something for Nothing" results were wrong. Everyone had seemed so happy when Professor Fox was interviewed on *Talk Right*. A week or so later, the editorial that mentioned Professor Fox and CROSS appeared in the *Wall Street Journal*. A framed copy of that editorial was on the wall in Dr. Crocker's office. What would happen if he told Dr. Crocker that the results presented in "Something for Nothing" were wrong? Dr. Crocker would probably write a letter to the *Wall Street Journal* to correct the mistaken impression conveyed in the editorial. But, while that would be the honorable and Christian thing to do, it would not be easy or pleasant.

He had almost convinced himself that he was about to be fired as he entered Dr. Crocker's office. Much to his surprise and his relief, Dr. Crocker greeted him warmly, even coming around from behind his desk to shake his hand.

"Greg, you've been doing some really fine work for us here."

"Thank you, Dr. Crocker, I appreciate the opportunity you've given me."

"'Something for Nothing' is only the start for CROSS. You've proved that you have a good nose for sniffing out research. You're a regular research bloodhound. So we've decided to send you to the American Economic Association annual meeting in Boston. All expenses paid."

He was amazed at his good fortune. He had wanted to attend the annual economics convention ever since he'd started graduate school, but simply couldn't afford it.

"Thank you, sir. Thank you very much."

"No need to thank me. This is not charity. We want you to do some work for us up in Boston."

"Sir?"

"There will be thousands of economists at this convention, and hundreds and hundreds of papers presented. You did such a fine job of finding 'Something for Nothing,' we would like you to go hunt us up some more research. Go to the sessions, find some papers that we can publish in our *CROSS Currents* series. Talk to those folks, tell them about the fine opportunities they could have to get their work publicized with CROSS, just as David Fox did."

He felt a little queasy as he thought of his recent discovery about "Something for Nothing." Crocker did not notice.

"Sir, I'm not used to going up to strangers and introducing myself."

"This is as good a time as any for you to develop that skill. Just remember, you are serving as CROSS's agent and representative at these meetings. And as such, you need to present yourself well. So we here at CROSS got a little present for you."

Crocker reached back onto his desk and picked up a small package wrapped in red and green paper. "Merry Christmas, Greg."

Greg was shocked. "Thank you very much, Dr. Crocker."

He unwrapped the present, careful not to tear the paper. The giftwrap covered a paper box, and inside this box was a silver object, with "Greg Shankle, CROSS" inscribed on it. He took it out and discovered it was a business card holder. He opened it, and inside was a small stack of business cards with the CROSS logo, and which read "Greg Shankle/Senior Researcher/Center to Research Opportunities for a Spiritual Society/greg.shankle@ save.edu."

"Dr. Crocker, I don't know what to say."

"Greg, when you're up there in Boston, you'll need to show those economists that you're part of a serious organization. This will help you make a good impression on them."

"Thank you so much."

"You're welcome, son. Thank you for all you've done for CROSS. Now Pamela has your flight and hotel information. Check with her when you leave."

With that, he left Crocker's office. He stopped at Pamela Winship's desk, and she held up a large envelope. "Greg, this has your flight information and the information about the hotel where you will be staying. I also included a reimbursement form for you to fill out for your meals and any other incidental expenses. Please save all your receipts. I hope you have a good trip." She handed him the envelope, and then picked up a long box on her desk and smiled as she handed it to him. "Here are four hundred business cards, for when you run out of the ones in that new silver case." He took the envelope and the box. "Thank you, ma'am." He realized that this was the most Ms. Winship had ever spoken to him at one time and also the first time she had ever smiled at him.

He thought of that smile as he sat in the hotel lobby in Boston, but then, considering the mission he was on, redirected his attention to the guidebook containing the conference program. He took a pen out of the inside pocket of his blue blazer and began to check off sessions that looked promising. If he hurried, he could make the session "Religion and Economic Perfomance," which was being held at 10:00 in the Carl Yastrzemski Room at the Marriott Hotel. In the afternoon, there was a 2:00 session in the William Bulger Room of the Hilton entitled "What Does Abortion Do?" Tomorrow, Greg could start the day by attending the session "The Economics of Creationism" held in the Make Way for Ducklings Room at the Westin Hotel.

Greg continued to page through the program, and, seeing all the offerings, he wished he could be in two or three places at one time. He would also want a chance to visit the gallery where publishers showed their wares. As he began to write down a schedule on a pad of paper, he was careful to keep an hour open on Saturday afternoon when, just before he was to go to the airport for his return flight, he had arranged to meet with David Fox in the lobby of the Marriott. It was a meeting that he looked forward to with decidedly mixed emotions.

Chapter 27

The first two days of the conference had gone well for David. After his interview with Grindle, he spent the rest of Thursday meeting with the search committees from five other colleges. Friday was similarly busy, with six interviews. Each of the interviews seemed successful. There was some discussion about his teaching experience in almost all of the interviews, and questions about the prospects for his dissertation chapters becoming journal articles in most cases. One common theme of all the interviews was "Something for Nothing." This was not so surprising, since he'd included the clipping from *USA Today* in his application packet. Beyond this, almost all of the interviewers had seen the *Wall Street Journal* opinion piece, and a few had heard the radio interview with Alan Glidden.

The painful experience of the last year had taught him, however, that seemingly good interviews may not lead to making the short list and being given the opportunity to visit campuses on fly-outs in later January and February. Still, this time, many of the interviews ended with the professors on the search committee saying things like "We look forward to continuing this discussion in a few weeks," or "We think you'll really like our campus," phrases he had not heard the year before.

After his last interview on Friday, reflecting on the differences in the experience across the two years, he thought about the role "Something for Nothing" played in the apparent change in his fortunes. Economists work in areas that should inform policy, and sometimes their research actually does. The chance that any one paper has a perceptible impact on policy, however, is pretty small. The professors on the search committees, all of whom were older than David, seemed impressed that, at his tender age, his work had influenced the public debate. Furthermore, professors' favorable impression of the attention paid to "Something for Nothing" did not seem to be affected by their own political leanings. Professor Sollock of Hampshire College, clearly a liberal, as well as Professor Dover of Pepperdine University, whose conservative stripes were as obvious as the hairpiece he wore, both showed the same levels of enthusiasm for the publicity accompanying his work. They, and all the other interviewers, seemed anxious to tap into that publicity for their own school. Some even mentioned how their deans reward media attention, and that exposure like that gained by "Something for Nothing" would greatly benefit their departments in the never-ending struggle for scarce resources within the college.

David had been so busy on Thursday and Friday that he hesitated before deciding to go to the reception hosted by Columbia for its faculty, students, and alumni on Friday evening. His hesitation had to do with his fatigue after two days filled with interviews. Earlier in the fall, when he was considering attending this reception, he'd had second thoughts about sending in his RSVP for a different reason, one that involved a comparison between his situation and those of a number of his classmates who had landed tenure-track positions. In light of the last two days, however, this concern now seemed moot.

He found his way to the Larry Bird Room of the Hilton where the Columbia reception was being held. He entered the room and went straight to the cash bar, both to have something to hold in his hand and to help him unwind after a day filled with interviews. After plunking down $6 for a Heineken, he turned and looked for a familiar face. His eyes met those of Professor Standwell, who showed no glimmer of recognition that this was a student in his Monetary Theory class four years ago. David made no effort to rekindle their relationship. Glancing to his right, David saw Professor Alton, a younger man who he always considered very nice, and not just in comparison to the other faculty (which was a pretty low bar). Professor Alton saw David and greeted him.

"David, how are you?"

"I'm fine, Professor Alton, thanks. How are you?"

"Great. By the way, now that you have your PhD, you should be calling me Joe, not Professor Alton."

"Oh, okay Joe."

"Where are you now?"

"I've got a one-year visiting appointment at Kester College. But I'm interviewing at a lot of places for a tenure-track job."

"Good luck. You got mentioned in that editorial in the *Journal*, right?"

David looked at his one-time teacher to see if he was judging him harshly. It did not appear so.

"Yeah, it seems like that's what I'll become famous for."

"Well, at least you'll become famous for something."

"Right now, I'd settle for a job."

"I bet you have a good shot."

"Thanks, Joe."

"Take care, David. I hope the interviews go well."

"Thanks, see you."

David looked around for someone else to talk to, now that Joe had moved on. He saw Maria Lopez-Schneider, a student who had begun graduate school with him, drinking a glass of red wine next to the cash bar. He had heard, secondhand, that she now taught at the University of Michigan. They were not especially friendly during their years at Columbia, though he had admired her from afar, as did all the other male graduate students, and probably some of the younger professors. It was obvious why, given how stunning she looked tonight. No sensible pantsuit for her: she wore a little black dress. David noticed that she had cut her hair short. During his second year, in the Applied Econometrics course, he often sat behind Maria and lost track of the lecture whenever she took her then long hair in both hands and pinned it to the top of her head. He probably would have done better in that class if Maria didn't have such a lovely, graceful neck.

He had never spoken to her for more than a few minutes at a time during their years of study, and all those conversations, if that's what they could be called, were about class assignments or upcoming exams. But here she was, smiling at David, raising her wineglass toward him, and walking in his direction. He almost looked behind him to see who she was greeting. She stopped in front of him and gave him a big smile.

"David Fox, it's been a long time. How are you?"

"Great, thanks. How have you been, Maria?"

"Fine, really fine. Lots of work, you know. I presented papers at a couple of sessions today, and I'm discussing a paper at a session tomorrow. It just never seems to end, does it? It's nice to have a chance to unwind," she said, raising her wineglass and taking a big slug. "Are you presenting any of your work?"

"No, actually I'm interviewing. I'm really busy; I've got about twenty interviews."

"Twenty? That's great. I guess you've become a really hot ticket since your research got mentioned in the *Wall Street Journal*."

David was pleased she knew about this. "Oh, you saw that? It's a pretty interesting area, actually, and people on hiring committees like it when your work helps shape the public debate. Of course, nothing's certain about the job market, but I have a good feeling about how things are going this year."

"Good luck. Where are you now?"

"I'm teaching at Kester College, in upstate New York. It's a nice place, but I think I can do better."

"I'm sure you can."

"Thanks. You're at Michigan, right?"

"Yeah, good old Ann Arbor. I guess there's some benefit to lack of social opportunities; it helps keep me focused on my research."

While he was trying to figure out whether or not this was a joke that required some type of laugh in response, Maria drained her glass of wine. "I'm getting a refill, how about you?"

David had about half his beer left but quickly quaffed it down. "Sure, that sounds great. Maybe I'll go for wine this time, too."

They each got a glass of wine and walked over to the side of the room.

"How's your teaching and research going?" he asked as she sipped her new glass of wine.

"Too slowly," she answered. "Sometimes it feels like you're hitting your head against the wall. And all these grad students come by and ask me to be a reader on their dissertation."

"Hey, be nice to them. We were in that position just a year ago."

"I know, I know, and I feel like I shouldn't just blow them off, but there's so much I have to do for my own career. At least I don't have to do any teaching my first year."

"That's great."

"It is, but they expect a lot from you. They figure that if you're not teaching then you should have at least four or five papers finished and submitted by the end of the year. I've got a couple of papers done, but I really doubt I'm going to be producing at the rate they expect."

"Yeah, I'm finding it hard to get my research finished, too."

"But you're getting a reputation for your research already with that education paper. I didn't remember that was your area."

"It isn't, not really. Most of my current work is in environmental. I wrote that paper, the one that's getting all the press, for the second-year Applied Econometrics class."

"Oh, were you in that class that Paxton taught?"

"Yeah. Were you in that class, too?"

"I was. But I didn't write a paper that got mentioned in a national newspaper."

"You know, sometimes you just get lucky."

"I bet it's more than luck. Where did you send that paper?"

"I'm touching up some of the results, but I'm thinking of sending it to the *American Economic Review*. It would be nice to get a really good hit this early in my career."

"That would be nice. At Michigan, it seems that if you don't get a good hit early, then they think you've struck out." Maria laughed at her own effort at a baseball joke, and David laughed along, too. "Hey," she said, "my wine's gone. How about another glass?"

David had only had a few sips of his wine, but he quickly drank the rest to be accommodating. "Sure, but this time let me buy."

They each got another glass of wine, and then returned to their spot on the side of the room and leaned against the wall, a little closer to each other than they had been before. The reception had begun to thin out. The few people left in the room were probably current grad students, judging by their youth and their apparel.

"Is Kester College in a city?"

"No, it's in a nothing little town."

"It must get boring there."

"There isn't much to do. You can go into Albany, but it's not like there's that much to do there, either."

"Well, Ann Arbor is no Manhattan either."

"It must get lonely there."

"It does. I guess it must get pretty lonely in upstate New York, too."

David thought of Angie for the first time since the day before he arrived at the conference. "It can be that way."

But it doesn't have to be that way, does it? he reasoned.

"It's really pretty around there. It's not that far to the Adirondacks. You should come visit sometime, maybe to give a seminar or something."

"That would be nice."

"Great, I can talk to the department chairman. What week would work well for you?"

"I don't know, David, I'll have to check. Let's be in touch sometime in January."

"Okay, I guess I can find your e-mail address on the Michigan Economics web page."

"Sure, it's there. Listen, I have to go now, I've got to finish up my discussant comments for tomorrow."

"Yeah, me too. I have two more interviews tomorrow morning."

She took her wineglass, which was almost empty, and clinked it against his. "Good luck with those."

"Thanks, Maria. We'll be in touch."

"Ciao."

"Ciao, Maria."

Back in his room, he thought about Maria coming to give a seminar at Kester. Maybe if she gave a seminar on Friday she could stay for the weekend. Angie wasn't the only woman interested in him. And maybe he wouldn't even be in Knittersville next year, given how well all those interviews had gone. After two weeks dominated by sad thoughts about Angie, it was relief to think things were finally going well.

Chapter 28

David finished his last two interviews on Saturday morning, with the final one ending at noon. He was in no rush to leave the hotels where the meetings were being held. If he lingered around, he might run into some friends, or some of the people with whom he had interviewed, or Maria Lopez-Schneider. He had to stick around for a while anyway since he had committed to meet the student from CROSS, Greg Shankle, at 12:15. He was appreciative of what CROSS had done for him and was happy to meet with Shankle. But he hoped that this meeting wouldn't take too long.

David hated to be late for anything, and so he dashed from the Weston Hotel to the lobby of the Marriott as soon as he finished his interview with Hamilton College. As he walked into the lobby, he looked around in an effort to identify Shankle. It was pretty clear that the people who seemed to be over thirty were not Shankle. He also guessed that the younger fellow with the expensive suit was not Shankle, nor was the young man with the ponytail. He continued to scan the room.

"Professor Fox?"

He turned around and faced a short, slight man, a few years younger than himself, wearing a blue blazer, gray slacks, a white shirt, and a striped tie. A blue canvas conference bag, just like the one David had also received, was slung over his shoulder. The top line of the name tag on the blazer read "GREG."

"You must be Greg. Nice to meet you."

"It's an honor to meet you, Professor Fox."

"You can call me David. How have you been enjoying the conference?"

"Oh, it's been great, David. I've attended a lot of sessions. I even saw Samuelson walking around! That was pretty amazing."

"Yeah, it's fun to attend these conferences."

"Well, it's my first time and I'm really enjoying it. Have you been to a lot of sessions?"

"Actually, Greg, I've been pretty busy interviewing for jobs."

"Wow, that's great. I'm sure that lots of places would love to hire you."

The kid seemed okay. David had some time. Things had been going well. He felt magnanimous.

"Greg, would you like to have lunch? My treat."

"Oh, that would be nice, but let me buy lunch. I'm on an expense account from CROSS."

David agreed, amused by the idea that this kid, a graduate student, had an expense account. They went into the restaurant off the hotel lobby. As they waited for a seat, they chatted about the sessions that Greg had attended. David was struck by the fact that all of them seemed to have a religious theme, but he did not mention this.

The hostess showed them to a booth.

"Professor Fox, er, David, I really admire your work."

What a sweet kid. "Thank you Greg, that's very nice of you to say."

"The thing is though, it's wrong."

He did not think he heard Greg correctly. "Excuse me?"

Greg reached into the blue canvas conference bag and took out a sheath of papers. "You see, in the programs you sent me there's a mistake. Here, in this line, you should have written $j = 1$, n, but you had $i = 1$, n."

He took the papers that Greg handed him and looked at them. These were the programs he had sent Greg in late November. He had written these a couple of years ago and hadn't looked at them since. It would be impossible to recall all the details of the programs now. What did this guy know, anyway? He was a grad student at some crackpot institute.

He tried to use his most polite voice. "Thanks very much for pointing this out, Greg. I'll be sure to make these corrections in the next draft."

"The thing is, this mistake changes all your results. I already fixed the program, and when it's corrected nothing is significant anymore. The results don't hold."

He stared at Greg. Who was this guy? He seemed to be re-counting this with an air of sorrow, not one of triumph. Still, who was this guy?

"Can I help you?" asked the waitress.

"Oh, sorry, ma'am, just a second." Greg quickly scanned the menu and asked for a hamburger and a Coke. David said he would have the same.

After the waitress left, David leaned over the table and said in a low voice, "Greg, are you sure *you* didn't make a mistake?"

"Pretty sure, yeah. I checked this a couple of times, and each time I came up with the same answer."

"Well, if you're only pretty sure, maybe there isn't a mistake."

"Actually, David, I'm almost certain there's an error in your program."

"I don't know. Even if that's true, how could that one small change affect the results so much? It's just not logical."

"No, if you think it through, it's exactly what you would expect." He then went on to explain, calmly and in great detail, how the resampling properties of the program changed completely with this mistake. And, with the change in the resampling, the standard regression assumptions are violated. Once that happens, the results become very sensitive to small changes in the values of the variables. So it really wasn't surprising that the results changed so much with this one, seemingly small, mistake.

David lost the train of the argument once Greg started talking about the violation of the standard assumptions. Apparently, he had spent too much time in Applied Econometrics looking at Maria Lopez-Schneider's neck. But Greg didn't seem to have had any distractions affecting his ability to understand advanced econometrics. Even though David couldn't follow all of the details of the argument, it was evident that Greg really knew what he was talking about. Maybe he was enrolled in some crackpot program, but he was well trained in econometrics, in fact, better trained than he was. Furthermore, Greg seemed to have an intuitive feel for the statistical intricacies of the problem that David knew he himself did not possess.

Finally, Greg finished explaining how his program, indeed his entire paper, was incorrect.

"Greg, who else have you told about this?"

"No one, David."

"You went to all this work, and you didn't share it with anyone, not your friends, not your professors?"

"I wanted to tell you first. At first, I thought maybe you could show me that I had made a mistake, or you would explain how

I overlooked something. But then, once I realized I was right, I thought it was only fair to talk to you before I told anyone else."

He stared at Greg. Was he taunting him? Was he playing up his superior understanding of statistics? Was he resentful of his Columbia degree?

"Are you going to tell anyone else?"

"Well, first I want to see if I can do something different that would save your results. I have a couple of ideas that might work."

"I guess we would be coauthors then," David said with a bit more edge to his voice than he had intended.

Greg looked down at the table as he replied, "No, that wouldn't be right. It was your idea and your data. If my ideas work out, well, it's just like I made a couple of minor suggestions."

"Greg, I didn't mean anything by that, I'm sorry. Look, if you find out how to fix the problem, I'd be proud to have you as a coauthor. Besides, "F" comes before "S" in the alphabet, so I'd still be first author."

Greg looked up and smiled at him. It was a sweet smile, he thought. He decided that Greg wasn't out to sink his career; he was honestly concerned about research being correct.

"Let's both think about this and be in touch in a couple of weeks."

"Sure, that's fine. I have to leave now anyway, since my flight leaves in about two hours." Greg reached down and pulled a silver box out of his jacket pocket. He took a business card from the box and slid it across the table to him.

"Here's my card, in case you want to contact me."

"Thanks, Greg. Thanks very much."

Greg called for the check and paid for lunch with cash. He got a receipt from the waitress and gathered his things.

"I still admire your work. It's just that there seem to be some errors."

He stared at Greg's back as he walked away. When he got to the door of the restaurant, Greg turned around and waved to him. He weakly waved back.

Chapter 29

David returned to Knittersville on Sunday, the day after the conference ended. He left his parents' house mid-afternoon, and drove due west on the Massachusetts Turnpike, toward the sunset that turned the low clouds red, then purple. The clouds darkened as the sun sank below the horizon, becoming a shade of indigo slightly darker than the open sky around them. He listened to rock stations, switching from one to another as the signals faded. In Western Massachusetts, with no good stations coming in, he switched the radio off and began to sing to himself. He was a little startled when, somewhere between the Westfield and Lee exits, he realized he had been singing, "You can't always get what you want / But if you try sometime / You get what you need."

He knew that there was little chance that he, or any other interviewees, would get exactly what they wanted and hear from schools in the week immediately following the conference. This did not stop him from checking his e-mail every hour or so during that week. But this understanding of the way the process worked did make him less concerned, at least at an intellectual level, while his inbox remained free of correspondence about fly-outs during that week.

He did remain concerned, however, about his conversation with Greg and the veracity of the results in "Something for Nothing." Monday, his first full day back in Knittersville, he got up early and began to review the programs and the data he had sent to Greg. He spent most of that day trying to reconstruct the way he had addressed the problem four years ago. By the early evening, he figured out the logic behind what he had done and was able to replicate his original results.

Getting up early on Tuesday morning, David turned his attention to Greg's critique. After a couple of hours of working through the programs, he saw Greg's point. Then, making the corrections suggested by Greg, he found that, just as Greg said, the original results were completely changed.

By early afternoon, he needed a break. He got his suit, towel, and goggles and went to the pool. He was the only one in the locker room, and, but for the lifeguard, the only one in the swimming area. The lifeguard briefly looked up from his paperback novel when he entered the pool, and then returned to the murder mystery. David swam in long, steady strokes. He occasionally lost track of how far he had swum ("Was that 600 or 650 yards?"). When this happened, he always took the shorter distance as the correct one.

He decided to stop by the Economics Department after his swim to check his mail. As he walked down the corridor of Central Hall, he saw Professor Wellingham walking toward him, dressed in a long overcoat and wearing a fedora.

"Fox, Happy New Year to you."

"Thank you, Professor Wellingham. Happy New Year to you as well."

"Our paths failed to cross very often during the fall, but I've heard some good things about your classes. Well done, Fox, keep it up."

"Thank you, Professor."

"I assume you were at the meetings in Boston. I trust they went well."

"I had a lot of interviews. I thought I did okay."

"I'm sure you did. From what I understand from Stern, you may have many opportunities. I hope that you keep us in mind as you're gallivanting around visiting campuses. We are hiring, you know. I think Stern will be in touch with you."

"Thank you, sir. That would be a nice."

"Of course, we need to bring in others to interview as well. Process and all that."

"I understand."

"Well, good luck to you, Fox. Happy New Year."

"Thanks, Professor. Happy New Year to you, too."

David found a bunch of glossy flyers in his mailbox, some departmental announcements, and an invitation to a Christmas party held a few days after he had left Knittersville for his parents' house. He threw everything away. He would start the year with a clean slate.

He decided to stop by Jeff White's office on his way out, on the off chance that Jeff was there. He was surprised, and pleased, to see Jeff's door ajar. He knocked on the door.

"Yes?"

"Hey, Happy New Year."

"Hey!" Jeff said, rising to give David a hug. "Happy New Year to you. What happened to you? You just sort of disappeared in December. I thought you might have decided to move to the University of Cancun or something."

"Yeah, I know, sorry about that. I decided to leave pretty suddenly in December, after Angie and I had a fight. I went to stay with my parents for a couple of weeks, and then I was at the meetings."

"Did you and Angie break up?"

"I'm not sure. She said we should take some time off until the new year. But I haven't spoken with her since we fought."

"I'm sorry. Maybe it will work out."

"Maybe."

"Are you going to call her?"

"Not yet. I'm not sure she wants me to. And besides, I'm really busy right now."

"Are you? What happened at the meetings?"

"The interviews went really well. I think I may get a few fly-outs."

"You know, they seem to be interested in you here, also."

"I know. I just saw Wellingham in the hall. But I got some bad news also, and I'm a little worried."

He told Jeff about his meeting with Greg, and his efforts that week to figure out what he might have done wrong and whether Greg was right. He also mentioned how the people who interviewed him seemed especially interested in "Something for Nothing," and his fear that, if the results in this paper proved wrong, any interest in him would evaporate. Jeff listened quietly, and then turned and looked out the window at the snowy field outside.

"David, I think you're going to have to publish an erratum that shows the right result, or withdraw your paper. You know, all we really have as professors is our reputations. If people find out that you made a mistake, that can be a problem. But it's a much bigger problem if people find out that you made a mistake and then you tried to cover it up."

"This might be my only chance to land a tenure-track job!"

"Suppose you did get a job, but then people find out that you were lying about your results. That would be worse, wouldn't it?"

"I guess."

"And besides, David, it's just wrong."

"I know, but I was so close."

"You are so close. That was just one paper. You have other papers, you have stuff from your dissertation. Polish those papers, get them ready for your fly-outs. You're a good teacher, and your research has promise. Even without "Something for Nothing," I bet you'll get what you want."

"And if I don't," David said in a resigned tone, "I'll get what I need."

Subject: Visit to Brunsfield College
Date: 1/11/2008, 1:10 PM
To: David Fox <david.m.fox@kester.edu>
From: Linda Goldman <lgoldman03@brunsfield.edu>

Dear David,

Danny Rodriguez and I enjoyed meeting with you at the AEA meetings in Boston. We were impressed by your credentials, and, after our interview, we decided that you would be a good fit for the Economics Department at Brunsfield College. We would like to invite you to come here for a full-day interview during which you will meet with all of our economics professors as well as with our students and our provost.

Could you please contact our department secretary, Ms. Helen Wilkins, to set up a date for you to visit Brunsfield? You can reach Ms. Wilkens at (207) 555-2960. She will assist you with your travel arrangements and your reservation at the Brunsfield Guest House on the campus of the college. If you can arrive early enough on the day before the interview, we would be very pleased to take you out to dinner that evening. You can plan on leaving Brunsfield late in the afternoon on the day of your interview, which should give you enough time to catch a flight back.

We look forward to your visit.

Yours,
Linda
Professor Linda Goldman
L.L.Bean Foundation Professor of Economics

Chapter 30

David flew from Albany to Portland on a small prop jet that had twenty-four seats. The plane left Albany in the early afternoon, rising above the snow-covered hills near the airport and then eventually leveling off as it crossed the Berkshire Mountains. He had planned to review the PowerPoint slides for his presentation, but his seat was too narrow, and too close to the seat in the row in front of him, to use his laptop comfortably. So, instead, he gazed out the window at the forests of New England and then, as the plane began its descent over the coast of Maine, at the Atlantic Ocean.

His overnight bag had been taken out of the cargo hold and was on a large cart next to the airplane as he disembarked. The door from the runway led directly into the main room of the terminal. As he entered the terminal, he saw a man in a black watch cap and a plaid woolen jacket holding a hand-lettered sign with his name on it. He went over to the man and introduced himself.

"I'm David Fox."

"Mr. Fox, I'm your driver, Rusty. I'll be taking you up to Brunsfield College. The limousine is this-a-way. Would you like me to take your bag?"

David was rolling his small bag behind him. "No, that's okay."

"It's actually part of my job, Mr. Fox."

"It's fine, Rusty. I can just wheel it behind me."

"Suit yourself," Rusty said, and, turning on his heel, walked ahead of David into the parking lot.

David followed Rusty, who pulled a set of keys out of his coat pocket and unlocked the door of a minivan.

"Is this the limousine?"

"Yep."

David opened the sliding door and sat down in one of seats in the middle row. Rusty pulled out of the airport parking lot, past a number of shopping malls, and onto the Maine Turnpike heading north. After driving in silence for fifteen minutes, Rusty pulled the van onto Route 1 North, and they continued up the coast.

David, feeling a little bad about denying Rusty the opportunity to fulfill his job obligations back in the terminal, leaned forward from his seat in the middle of the van and asked, "Have you lived in Maine your whole life?"

"Not yet."

He reconsidered his desire to converse and looked out the window as they continued traveling up the coast of Maine. After another twenty minutes, Rusty pulled the minivan onto the campus of Brunsfield College. The campus was beautiful, with old, three-story fieldstone buildings and modern buildings that complemented the college's architectural heritage. The snow sparkled under the late January sun. Rusty pulled up to one of the fieldstone buildings and stopped the van.

"This here's the Economics Department." Rusty said. "Hope you enjoyed your trip today with Downeast Limousine Service."

"Thank you, Rusty. I can get the bag myself."

With that, David opened the door and got out of the minivan. The old façade of the building belied the complete modernization of its interior. As he entered the building he could see, through a glass wall, the Economics Department office across from him. The department secretary, sitting at a modern workstation that would not have looked out of place in an investment bank, smiled and greeted him.

"You must be Professor Fox. I'm Helen Wilkins. Welcome to Maine and to Brunsfield College."

"Thank you very much. It's a beautiful campus."

"We like it. Professor Goldman is expecting you."

Helen led David down the hall to a corner office. She knocked on the door, opened it, and said, "Professor Goldman, Professor Fox is here."

Linda Goldman rose from behind her desk and, removing her glasses, crossed her office to greet David. It was a beautiful office, with floor-to-ceiling bookcases, large windows that looked out onto the snow-covered quad, and an oriental rug. Linda invited him to sit at one of the two chairs next to a small table, and she sat down across from him.

"David, welcome to Brunsfield. We're so glad that you were able to come."

"Thank you, Professor Goldman."

"Please call me Linda. You'll be staying in the campus guesthouse tonight. Helen will walk you over there in a few minutes. You can rest for a while, and then Danny Rodriguez and I would like to take you out to dinner at around 6:00."

"That would be very nice, thank you."

Linda handed him the sheet of paper that had been on the table. "Here's your schedule. Tomorrow morning, some of our students will meet you at the guesthouse, and then take you out to breakfast at a student cafeteria on campus. There are meetings scheduled with other faculty members, including a lunch. Your seminar will be in the early afternoon. Then, before we take you to the airport, there is a meeting with the dean. I'm afraid that we're not giving you a lot of free time."

"That's okay. I'm glad to be here."

They shook hands, and he left the chairwoman's office. Helen Wilkins walked him across campus to the guesthouse, handing him a key for his room. The room included a single bed, a desk, a nightstand, and a bureau. He hung up his coat and turned his laptop on. Over the next hour, he reviewed the slides for his upcoming seminar.

His phone rang a few minutes after 6:00. It was Linda Goldman, waiting in front of the guesthouse. He turned off his computer, put on his coat, went outside into the dark early evening, and got into the waiting Volvo. The seat warmer on the passenger side was on, and he felt the soothing heat through his coat.

Linda and David had a pleasant conversation during their drive on the harshness of the weather in Maine at this time of year, and the reward for that, which was the very pleasant summer weather. David realized that, subtly, Linda was selling the college's location.

Danny Rodriguez was waiting for them inside the entrance of "100 Shore Drive," which had been converted from a large Victorian residence into one of the best restaurants in Southern Maine, according to the laminated article next to the maître d's desk. The three were shown to their table and given menus. David, used to the modest fare at the Cask and Barrel, was impressed by the offerings here. But he remembered this was work, and not recreation, so he avoided salads (easy to have small bits of lettuce stuck to your teeth) and the linguine (potentially sloppy). Instead, he went for the Chilean Sea Bass with Tomato and Avocado Salsa, deciding that it was a good compromise between what he most preferred to eat and what he could eat with the least risk of embarrassing himself. Danny ordered from the wine list.

The pleasant tone of the conversation in the Volvo continued in the restaurant. There was some discussion about the Economics Department at Brunsfield ("We value teaching, but we also give our junior faculty time off to pursue their research interests"), living in the area ("There's so many outdoor activities here —David, have you ever tried sea kayaking?"), and the cultural attractions of Portland ("There's some really good theater, with Equity actors, and it doesn't cost you an arm and a leg for a ticket"). Linda and Danny asked about Kester and Knittersville. For reasons he didn't fully understand, David felt an obligation to discuss some of the most attractive aspects of the school ("Some of my students are really good.") and the town ("It isn't that far to a few nice ski areas.")

Over dessert, the conversation turned to David's own work. At first, Danny asked about the topic of the seminar the next day, and the three of them discussed some of the connections between his research on environmental economics and the published literature in the field. As the waiter came around to offer a refill of their cups of decaf, Linda said, "So you won't be discussing "Something for Nothing" tomorrow? That paper has gotten a lot of attention."

"Actually, that was just a paper that I wrote to fulfill a requirement for my Econometrics class in graduate school. My dissertation work, and the work I plan to do in the near future, is much more in the field of environmental economics."

"Really, you just did that paper for a class?" Danny said. "That's amazing, since it's gotten so much press."

The surroundings, the meal, the pleasant conversation, the wine, and the seeming camaraderie had put him at ease. Without making the same type of calculation he had considered when choosing his food that evening, he replied, "The funny thing is, Danny, that paper's wrong."

Linda and Danny both looked shocked. "What do you mean that it's wrong?" Linda asked, her voice having suddenly taken on a much darker hue.

David realized the import of what he had just said. "It turns out that there was an error in the coding. The results are not as strong as I had originally thought."

"When did you find this out?" asked Danny.

He found himself speaking much more quickly than he had before the dessert course. "Just recently, just very recently in fact. A friend of mine pointed this out to me. He's a really good econometrician, and he found the error. We're going to publish a correction. But, like I said before, this isn't really the focus of my work. It's just something that got some attention for a while but no one is really looking at it anymore."

Linda was not old enough to be his mother, but she was old enough to be the older cousin whose experience informed her advice to a favorite relative. She put down her coffee cup and leaned across the table slightly. "David, I like you. Let me offer some friendly advice, as someone who has been involved in hiring for a long time. Right now, you're getting some opportunities because of "Something for Nothing." But when people find out that paper is wrong, they could be very disappointed in you. In fact, they could be so disappointed that they don't see all of your potential. It would be a good idea to let people know, very soon, about which of your papers you yourself value, and which you don't."

It was quiet at the table for a few minutes after that. Linda requested the check, and the three diners turned their attention to their coffees. David and Linda said goodnight to Danny when they left the restaurant, then the two of them got into Linda's Volvo for the drive back to the Brunsfield campus.

"David," Linda said after a short time, and in a tone softer than the one she used at the conclusion of the meal, "I wasn't try-ing to be harsh back there, but I have to admit that I was surprised by your news. I really meant it when I said that you have a lot of potential. But no one likes to be a chump, and if you don't let people know about the error in your paper, they might feel that way once the news gets out. The best strategy for you is to let the people that you're interviewing with know ahead of time that you found a mistake, and that you're working to correct it."

"Thank you, Linda, that's good advice."

"Your real professional focus, environmental economics, is one that will be getting more attention over the next few years. Have you been interested in that field your whole career?"

"Not yet."

To his relief, Linda laughed.

Chapter 31

"Why did you become an economist?"

David looked across the breakfast table at Eric Samuels, a Brunsfield senior, and realized that no one had ever actually asked him that question before. Nor had he prepared an answer for it, the way he had prepped for questions about his teaching plans and research strategies. He knew that the students joining him for breakfast, Eric, Joy Cohen, and Amy Romero, did not really have a vote in the Economics Department's decision about whom to hire. They would just be asked whether they thought he would fit in well at Brunsfield. He guessed that the real reason for this breakfast with the best and the brightest students the department could muster was as much an effort to sell Brunsfield as was Linda Goldman's discussion the previous evening of Maine in the summer. Even more than Linda's descriptions, this breakfast had its desired effect; these were nice, smart, and engaging kids, and, apparently, ones who could come up with a good, direct, and trenchant question.

"I guess I wanted to put the concept of comparative advantage into practice."

"Did you always know that you wanted to be an economist?" Joy asked.

"Actually, I didn't start out as an economics major in college. In fact, I didn't know what I wanted to study. When I was little, I liked science, but my high school science courses were pretty boring and I lost interest by time I started college. I always followed current events, but the political science course I took in my freshman year of college was a little frustrating to me; there never seemed to be any concrete answers to questions. Then, when I took my first economics course, I saw that, for some questions at least, there were ways to get answers. I guess I found that pretty satisfying. The questions were about important things, too, like why people can't find jobs, or the reason that some people are poor while others are rich. And the way that the reasoning works in economics, trying to identify and then weigh benefits and costs, just seemed to match the way I thought about things. Maybe that's why I did really well in my economics courses throughout college."

"That's sort of how I feel about it, too," Joy said. "I mean the part about getting answers to important questions. It must be great to get even deeper into that when you start graduate school."

"The stuff you do in the first couple of years of graduate school is actually pretty different than what you guys are doing now. It's very heavy on math, and a lot of the time you can't see how these complicated and very technical models are linked to the real world."

"That must be hard," Amy said.

"Yeah, graduate school is difficult. I wouldn't necessarily recommend it. I was one of the best economics students in my year at college, but then at Columbia I was in the middle of the pack. That was a bit of a shock, after doing so well in college. But I managed to get through it and finish my dissertation."

"Columbia must be a lot different than Brunsfield," said Eric. "Would you want to be up here in Maine rather than in New York?"

David did not see the need to mention that the Columbia Economics Department was not rushing to offer him a tenure-track position. He could be honest with these kids, but he didn't need to make himself look bad, either.

"A place like Brunsfield is really attractive to me. I had a lot of fun teaching at Kester this last semester, and I imagine Brunsfield would be like that. There are people doing good research at lots of places, not just at the Ivies. And Maine seems nice—it's probably even warmer in the winter here on the coast than it is in upstate New York."

The three students seemed to appreciate this answer and, in fact, it pretty accurately represented his current thinking. The semester at Kester had made him reconsider his professional, and life, goals. A year ago, in the cauldron of the job market with other aspiring Columbia students, he shared the prevalent view from Morningside Heights that any place lower than a top twenty-five department represented a disappointing outcome. Realistically, however, there just weren't that many opportunities at top research universities, and there were a lot of bright, ambitious, hardworking people out there. In fact, a lot of them were at places like Kester or Brunsfield. The professors he met during the rest of the day were clearly smart. They asked good and incisive questions at his seminar in the afternoon. And, during his one-on-one meetings with them, he found that they had lives outside their jobs. In fact, the professors he met at Brunsfield, much like Jeff and Murray at Kester, seemed to have struck a pretty good balance between their jobs and the rest of their lives. They were engaged in their teaching and worked on research, but he also saw the family photos in their offices and noted the recreational and community activities they mentioned.

By the end of the day, he had begun to fantasize about moving to Maine. So he was a little disappointed when Linda Goldman provided no words of encouragement as they waited together for

for the car to take him back to the Portland airport. She wasn't discouraging either and, thankfully, made no mention of their conversation over dessert the previous evening. Her parting words, "We'll be in touch," conveyed little information. He knew that this was appropriate, given that the full department needed to deliberate and not all candidates had made the trip to Maine yet, but he was still a little deflated by her lack of obvious enthusiasm.

He spent the car ride back to the Portland airport reviewing the events of the day, trying to gauge his prospects at Brunsfield. The seminar went well, the professors seemed to like him and, despite himself, he began to grow hopeful about his chances. On the plane ride from Portland to Albany, staring out the small window of the plane, he indulged himself by considering the broader implications of an offer from Brunsfield. Did Brunsfield seem like a place where he could get research done? Did he want to live in Maine? If he moved here, would he get to Boston more often than he had this year? How long would it take to drive from Brunsfield to Knittersville to see Angie on weekends?

Whoa, where had that question come from? He was really getting way ahead of himself now. He had no reason to believe that Angie would have any interest in his location during a weekend next fall. He wasn't even sure that she had the least bit of interest in where he would be this coming weekend.

But David was interested in knowing Angie's whereabouts, even though he had tried to keep from thinking about this during the past few weeks. Avoiding this topic was not easy, but it helped that he had been caught up with interviews in Boston during the first week of the new year and, after that, wrestling with Greg's revelation about the accuracy of the results in "Something for Nothing." But increasingly, in the last week or so, he had wanted to call Angie and see where he stood. He had hesitated because he felt awkward about contacting her. He also was a little afraid of how the conversation might go. But now, with this trip to Brunsfield, he had some news and a good pretext for a call.

He got back to his apartment around 9:00. He went to the phone as soon as he took off his coat and put his suitcase down. Giovanna picked up on the third ring.

"Hello."

"Oh, hi, Giovanna. It's David Fox. Is Angie there?"

Giovanna didn't answer right away. "Angie isn't here right now."

"Will she be in later?"

"I don't think you should call back tonight. She might not be back until late. Then she's going out of town on a business trip tomorrow. Do you want me to tell her you called?"

"Yeah, please do."

"I will. But I'm not sure when she can call you back. She's going out of town."

"That's okay. You can tell her she doesn't have to call me back. Maybe I'll call her next week."

"Next week might be better. She'll be back at the end of the week. I'll tell her you called."

"Thanks, Giovanna. See you around."

"Good night, David." Then, after a pause, "I'm sorry."

What did that mean? He wondered where Angie might be, and why she wouldn't be home until late. He thought about how awkward it might be to call her next week if his fears were, in fact, well founded.

After a few minutes, he took out his address book, looked up another number, and dialed it.

"Hello?"

"Hi, Maria, it's David, David Fox, calling from New York. How are you?"

Maria Lopez-Schneider sounded surprised. "David, hi, what's new?"

"Not much. I'm in the middle of the job market. I just got back from Maine. I had an interview at Brunsfield College."

"Oh, good for you. There are some nice opportunities at those small liberal arts places. I'm sure that they would be happy to have you there."

"I hope so. I think it went pretty well."

"Good. Good luck with that."

"How are things in Ann Arbor?"

"Busy. I'm teaching a grad course this semester, and it's taking a lot of time to prepare for it. I'm also trying to get a paper done for a conference in a couple of weeks. And, you know, all the other stuff, a couple of referee reports, some administrative stuff, advising students."

"Been doing any fun stuff?" David asked, but immediately regretted how silly the question must have sounded to Maria.

"No, not really. I'm pretty swamped."

"I guess you're too busy to come give a seminar at Kester."

"Oh, that's nice of you to ask. I really don't have time this spring. Maybe next year."

"Okay. Of course, I'm not sure I'll be here next year."

"Oh, right. Well, let's keep in touch about that. Let me know what happens."

"Sure."

"Okay, David, gotta go now. Take care, and good luck."

"Thanks Maria. Good luck to you, too."

"Thanks. Bye."

"Good-bye," said David. He hung up the phone and, suddenly exhausted from his trip, stripped off his clothes and climbed into bed without even unpacking his suitcase.

Chapter 32

Spring semester seems misnamed when it begins at Kester College. Snow covers the ground, the temperature is often in single digits, and the sun sets well before the staff leaves the college at 5:00. In upstate New York in late January, there is nothing to suggest the renewal typically associated with spring. But, in fact, the beginning of the second semester is a time of new classes, and new opportunities for both professors and students.

Fortunately, not everything in the spring semester was going to be new for David. The Principles of Economics course he was scheduled to teach would be close to identical to the one he offered in the fall semester. This meant much less time he'd have to devote to preparing classes in January and February as compared to September and October. It also meant that he could avoid some of the pedagogic mistakes he made in the fall; for example, he had already planned to begin this course with demand and supply diagrams rather than with examples drawn from *Freakonomics*. His other spring semester class, Environmental Economics, would not require too much preparation time either. David had served as a teaching assistant for an undergraduate Environmental Economics course when he was at Columbia, and, with great foresight, had taken careful class notes in anticipation of teaching the same course on his own someday. Kester students who signed up for Professor Fox's Environmental Economics course would be taking essentially the course taught to Columbia undergraduates by Professor Kane. The only difference, as far as David could see, would be that the Kester students would be spared Professor Kane's puns and feeble attempts at humor.

One responsibility that carried over from the fall to the spring semester was advising senior honors theses. As the new year began, and especially after the evening he returned from Brunsfield, David did not think of this so much as an obligation as an opportunity to continue to meet with Jenny Lake each week. The shot glass she gave him was moved to a place of prominence on his desk the day after he got back from Brunsfield and, since then, he found himself glancing at it often as he finished getting materials together for the semester that would begin tomorrow.

In fact, he has looking at the shot glass when he heard a knock on his office door and, after saying "Come in," saw Jenny enter his office.

"Hi, welcome back. How was your break?" he asked her enthusiastically, rising out of his chair.

She entered, smiling, and closed the door behind her. "It was great. I went skiing in Vermont for a week, and got to visit with my friends from high school who were home on break. Don't worry, I did some work on my thesis, too."

She then held her arms open to greet him, starting in where they left off in December. David stepped forward and gave her a hug. After a few moments, he stepped back and sat down, motioning to the chair facing him, offering her a seat.

"What courses are you taking this semester?"

"The thesis counts for a course, and I'm taking your Environmental Economics course, for sure."

"Good, I'm glad."

"Me too. It should be really interesting, especially since my thesis is about recycling. Since it's my last semester, I also want to take some fun courses, like this one on the French cinema. I'm not sure what else."

"Well, I hope you find something good."

"Thanks. How was your break?"

"Good, busy. I went to the economics convention and had lots of job interviews. Those went well."

"It would be awful for Kester if you left."

"It's nice of you to say that."

"No, really, I mean it. Over the break, I was thinking a lot about last semester, and I realized that your Social Issues class was the best course I've had here."

"Thanks, thanks very much, Jenny. You did really well in that class."

"And the work on my thesis, you know, you really helped me. I never had a chance to do research like that before. You were so patient and so good at explaining things."

"It was fun working with you. You really pick stuff up quickly. You're very smart, you know."

"That's sweet of you to say."

"No, really, you are."

"Well," she said, "you just can't leave Kester."

"I may not have a choice."

"Why don't you let them know that you've already got an official school shot glass," she said, pointing to her gift on his desk.

"Still unused."

"Really?" she asked, and stood up to pick up the glass off the desk to inspect it. This required her to lean over David as she reached for the glass. David leaned back in his chair, but he couldn't lean back far enough to avoid having Jenny brush against him as she reached for the glass. Still leaning over him, she turned to face him and said, "You should give it a try."

He did. He reached up and, with his arms around her neck, gave Jenny a kiss on the mouth. She didn't pull away. In fact, she kissed back. "This is amazing," he thought, as he stood and took her in his arms, kissing her still. "She's so gorgeous," he thought, as his hand slid down her back. "She's so hot," he thought, as their mouths opened and their tongues intertwined. "She's a student," he thought, and quickly broke their embrace and stepped back.

"What's wrong?" Jenny asked.

"This isn't right. We can't do this."

"I'm an adult."

"But you're my student. It's just not right."

"What if I don't take your class this semester?"

"No, Jenny, that's not it. It's not right no matter what."

"What, are you seeing somebody else?"

"Yes, er, no, I mean, not really. I'm not really sure. But even if I wasn't, it's just wrong for a professor to get involved with a student."

"Why?"

"I could get fired."

"So you won't do it because you're afraid?"

"No, it's not just that. Look, you're really beautiful and smart and nice. But think about what this would look like. No one would ever think that you earned any grade you got from me or from any of my friends on the faculty. Even if you never ever got any special treatment, no one would believe it."

"I know lots of other students who sleep with their professors."

"Lots?"

"Well, okay, not lots, but some. And no one says that they get special treatment."

"Even if that were true, Jenny, and I bet it's not, it's still wrong. I'm sorry, I'm really sorry, but I just can't do this."

She stared at him, and her eyes filled. Beautiful green eyes, the color of a lake, the eyes that first helped him tell the difference between her and the other Jenny. He wanted to tell her he'd made a mistake, it wasn't wrong, how could it be wrong? But he didn't say anything else.

Nor did she. Without another word, she picked up her coat, jerked open the door, and left his office.

He watched her go, thankful that no one else was in the hall at that moment. His heart was still beating hard, and he could still feel the sensation of her lips against his, and her body pressing against him. He wished that he did have a bottle in his office so he could finally use the shot glass.

"You did what?"

Jeff and David were in the Cask and Barrel, in a booth in the back. The bar was almost empty, since it was only 4:30 on a weekday.

"I didn't do anything. Well, practically nothing. I mean, she threw herself at me. She leaned over and put her tits right in my face, and I couldn't help it."

"But nothing happened, right?"

"We kissed a little, but then I told her I couldn't do this."

"What did she say?"

"Nothing. She just left. She seemed pretty upset."

Jeff sat for a minute, looking at David. "This is not good."

"Oh, thanks for that telling insight."

"Hey, you're the one who came to my office, told me we really had to go get a drink, and then asked for my advice."

"Jeff, I'm really sorry, I didn't mean it. It's just that I really fucked up."

"Look, you didn't fuck up that much, only a little. You would have really fucked up if you'd let it go further. Do you think she'll tell anyone?"

"How would I know? Don't they always?"

"No," Jeff said, looking down at his beer, "not always."

"What?"

"They don't always tell."

"How would you know?"

"Look, David, a few years ago, I fucked up, too," Jeff said, still looking down at his half-finished beer. "There was this guy in my class, a senior, a sweet kid. He had just come out and was having a hard time dealing with it. Somehow he knew that I was gay, and he would come by my office to talk. I had been in that same situation, coming out in college. And I was alone here in Knittersville. I didn't know anyone. One thing led to another. But it didn't last, and he was really discreet. I don't think anyone ever knew." He looked up at David. "Not until today."

"Your secret's safe with me, don't worry. I won't breathe a word of this to anyone."

"It's good to finally tell someone. I haven't even told Mark. We all do the wrong thing sometimes, we're only human. The important thing is to have the courage to set things right."

"Or to have the luck that we don't have to," David thought.

Subject: RE: Fixing SfN
Date: 1/29/2008, 10:55 PM
To: Greg Shankle <Greg.shankle@save.edu>
From: David Fox <david.m.fox@kester.edu>

Hi, Greg,

Thanks very much for your e-mails. It's interesting that you think there might be some new econometric techniques that we could use to correctly estimate the effects of the abstinence programs. Let me know what happens with that.

Greg, I'm going to need to eventually withdraw my working paper from the *CROSS Currents* series. As you know, I'm interviewing for jobs this year. A couple of people have advised me that I could be really harmed in my job search if people think that I was trying to fool them with false results.

I do want to keep working with you on a revised version of the paper, but, with my interviews and the semester beginning in a couple of days, I don't have time to do much right now.

Let's try to touch base again soon. I hope everything is going well with you.

Yours,
David

Chapter 33

Greg loved math puzzles and had always been good at them. Part of his attraction to economics was that understanding some aspects of it, especially statistics and econometrics, was just like mastering a math puzzle. Greg's experience in college, and at SAVE, convinced him that he could figure out any of the technical economic problems presented to him in his coursework. So far, he had been right.

But Greg was not just a math geek; he also liked the moral dimension of economics. That was why he liked David's work (since their lunch together, and especially after all the e-mails they had exchanged over the past month, he had become comfortable referring to Professor Fox as David). The problem was, however, that the results in the original version of "Something for Nothing" were wrong.

It had not taken long for him to find the error in David's original program. But there was something else about the estimation that had bothered him, something that, at first, he had a hard time identifying. He spent a full week after his return from Boston consulting statistics and econometrics textbooks in an effort to clarify his thinking. He had written a couple of e-mails to David, but David seemed as puzzled as he was. In fact, he wasn't sure that David fully understood the points that he was trying to make; this, he concluded, was because he himself was a bit vague about the problem.

Then, late one night in mid-January, he suddenly had a clear conception of the problem that had plagued the estimation method of "Something for Nothing." The problem was a little like one in an advanced econometrics textbook that he had looked at a few days before, but there were enough differences between that problem and the one using David's data that it took a while for him to see the parallels. Once he made the connection, however, the solution to the problem using David's data was clear. He jumped up from the chair at his cubicle and yelled out "YES!" in a very loud voice. Had there been anyone else at CROSS that evening, they would have been startled by his outburst. They would have been even more startled by the sight of him dancing around for the next few minutes as the joy of his discovery moved him to near-religious ecstasy.

Greg spent the next day working out the details of his insight. He was worried that, as he did this, he might find that his initial intuition was incorrect. But the deeper he got into the solution, the more it became clear to him that he had been right on target.

His solution seemed to offer a new method for estimating certain types of equations with data sets like the one David had used in "Something for Nothing." He wasn't sure about the generality of his results, however. There was no one at CROSS who he could ask about this, or even anyone at SAVE. In fact, he did not know any high-level econometricians. So he decided to write a short synopsis of his findings and send them to the only econometrician he could identify who might be able to tell him whether his solution was useful beyond its application to David's data; Professor Moses M. Appelfeld of the University of California, Berkeley, the author of Greg's well-thumbed Advanced Econometrics textbook. He spent the better part of a morning writing out his findings in a form that he felt he could send to Professor Appelfeld. Once he had done this, he found the professor's e-mail address on the Berkeley Economics Department website, and included his results as an attachment in his message to him.

Figuring out the theory was one thing, but applying it to actual data was another. It took almost a week to write a computer program that could implement his technique, and then a couple more days to run the program with David's data. After a little debugging, the program ran. But the estimates were not what he had expected. His results showed that teenage abstinence programs actually raised pregnancy rates by a significant amount! How could that be? He ran the regressions again, dropping some variables in one specification and adding other variables in another, but the positive effect remained.

He went back to the original data set. He found that there was a variable that showed whether students were given instruction in sex education in the ninth and tenth grades. Looking at the statistics for this variable, he found that abstinence programs tended to replace sex education courses. He thought for a few minutes and then worked on including the sex education variable in the data set. Once this was completed, he used his new technique to estimate whether sex education affected pregnancy rates.

It did. It did a lot. Girls who had sex education classes in the ninth and tenth grades were eight times less likely to get pregnant in high school than girls who did not have these classes. Even if the girls had only one year of sex education, they were still three times less likely to get pregnant than girls who had no exposure to this subject in school. Teenage abstinence programs remained positively associated with higher pregnancy rates, even after controlling for the fact that schools that offered these programs tended not to offer sex education classes as well. And no matter what other variables were included, or were not included, these results held.

Greg slumped in his seat. It had been a long three weeks since he returned from Boston, and he had been working on this project nonstop. What did he have to show for all this work? Teenage abstinence programs seemed to be worse than useless; they actually seemed to be harmful. And sex education classes, the type of classes that people at CROSS thought schools had no right to offer, seemed to cut pregnancy rates. What would Dr. Crocker think? What should he say to him? What should he say to anyone? Was he responsible for telling the world that the policy that CROSS had advocated was wrong and even harmful? What should he do?

He looked at the bracelet on his wrist. *WWJA?* What Would Jesus *Advise?*

Subject: RE: Sex ed and abstinence
Date: 2/7/2008, 8:04 PM
To: Greg Shankle <Greg.shankle@save.edu>
From: David Fox <david.m.fox@kester.edu>

Hi, Greg,

The results that you sent me are really interesting. It actually makes more sense to me that sex education programs lower pregnancy rates and abstinence programs raise them than the other way around—see the paper "What Happens When We Talk About Sex?" by Lovelace and Reims (*Quarterly Journal of Economics*, 2002). They find that surveys suggest that students are more careful about sexual relations after sex ed instruction in schools. But your research is the first that I've heard of that shows effects on pregnancy rates, and also shows that abstinence programs have unintended consequences.

I think that, when you write this paper up, you could send it to a top journal, for no other reason than the new techniques you developed—but also, the results themselves are important. It was very nice of you to offer to include me as a coauthor. I want you to think about this some more—it's perfectly fine if you want to publish this yourself since you've worked so hard on it. But, if you'd like, I would be willing to help you write it up and put the results in the context of the existing literature. My only stipulation to my involvement is that your name should come first in the author list since this is really your work.

I'm sorry to hear that you're worried about what the people at CROSS will think of all this, and that you might lose your research position there. If it would be helpful, you can tell Dr. Crocker to write to me about this; I'd be willing to take the blame in order to help you out.

Yours,
David

Chapter 34

The new year brought a number of new opportunities for Bill Crocker. Most of the media attention about "Something for Nothing" had died down by Christmas, but there was still a trickle of interest in the article, mostly from small local newspapers. Even though interest in that one particular *CROSS Currents* working paper was fading, interest in CROSS itself was on the ascent. Editors from both *Good News!* and the *Liberty Review* had contacted him about doing cover stories on the new Christian think tanks, stories that would prominently feature CROSS. Crocker was encouraged. But he had been in the public relations business long enough to know that there was a wide gulf between an exploratory discussion about an article and having a photographer come by for a cover shoot.

Bob Dronin, however, did not fully understand that there was a high ratio of exploratory ideas to articles published, and Crocker felt no need to convey this point to him in their phone conversation a few days before Christmas. Dronin was very pleased to see his investments in CROSS realize such high returns. He called one morning, a couple of days before Christmas.

"This is really good news, Bill, really good. You've given me a wonderful Christmas present this year."

"Thank you, Bob. I like to think of our work this fall as a present for the whole nation, since it gives such a powerful, positive message to the parents and youth of our country." ("Oh, you're good Crocker, you're very good," Bill thought to himself.)

"Well said, Bill. I think we are making some very nice progress, and some of my friends in Washington think so, too. I'd like to invite you to my place in West Palm Beach in early February, if your schedule is open then. I'm having a few people come by for golf and good fellowship. Skip Smith said he'll probably be able to join us."

Wilberforce Smith, the secretary of health and human services? Despite his best efforts, Crocker could not help sounding like an eight-year-old who had just found a new puppy under the Christmas tree when he replied, "Wow, that would be great!"

"Yea, you know Skip's a heck of a golfer, but not quite as good as he thinks he is," Dronin laughed. "But then again, who is?"

He laughed along with Dronin. "Bob, that would be fine. I'd be honored to visit you in Florida. I'll have my secretary Pamela contact your office."

"That secretary of yours still so pretty?"

"That she is, Bob."

After he hung up the phone, he looked out his window at the hills in the distance. He thought of how his fortunes had changed over the past month—and now, golf with Skip Smith! Things were moving in a good direction. He hadn't worked out any long-term master plan for his career—that would be foolish. Too many things tend to foul up long-term plans. On the other side, too many new, unforeseen opportunities present themselves that you can't plan for. But he was good at seeing opportunities, and then acting on them. Nimble, that's what he was. And brave, brave enough to seize a chance—carpe diem and all that.

His thoughts drifted from his own strengths to those of Pamela. Dronin was right, she was pretty. But she was more than that, she was smart. In some ways, Pamela was a kindred spirit. She, too, seemed to have a sense of possibilities, and a willingness to seize an opportunity.

After a few minutes of this reverie, he called Pamela into his office and told her about the call. His enthusiasm was infectious. Pamela told him that she was thrilled for him, and that she, too, thought this golf trip was a huge opportunity, one that might lead to a whole new set of opportunities for him. Here was a girl who could sense an opportunity. A very pretty girl who could sense an opportunity.

Pamela was not only pretty but also efficient. Even though it was only two days before Christmas, she was able to make all the arrangements for his travel to Florida by noon.

The next morning, Pamela came into Crocker's office.

"Bill, I'm going to take off now. I'm traveling to my sister's house in Washington for Christmas. But before I go, I got you this present."

He came from around his desk and took the envelope from Pamela.

"Go ahead, open it."

He opened the envelope, and tucked inside the card ("Let Us Celebrate the Birth of Our Lord") was a voucher for three golf lessons.

"Pamela, this is so thoughtful," he said.

"Well, when you're down in Florida with the secretary of health and human services, you don't want to be shanking your balls." They both laughed.

"Pamela, I got you a gift, too." He went to the desk and took out the small giftbox in his top drawer. (He had gone to a jewelery store yesterday afternoon to buy this for her. The clerk had said, "Your wife will love this," to which he replied, "This is a surprise for my wife.")

Pamela said, "Oh, Bill," as she opened the box and took out the necklace. "Here, help me put this on."

He stood behind her and clasped the necklace. She held her hair off her neck. Her hair smelled nice.

Pamela turned around and said, "Merry Christmas, Bill."

"Merry Christmas, Pamela." They hugged. She was thinner than Sally. They continued to hug. Her breasts pushed against his chest. He began to rub her upper back in small circular motions.

Pamela pulled away from him and, still holding his arms, said, "Bill, I think you are really going places. CROSS is lucky to have you. I hope we don't lose you soon."

"Pam, no matter where I go, I hope that we can still work together. You help me so much, and I only look good because of what you do."

Pamela laughed and stepped back. "You are too kind." She turned to leave. "You have a good Christmas now, you hear. Give my best regards to your family. I'll see you after New Year's."

What was that all about? He had, of course, noticed Pamela's looks before; to be truthful, that was one of the factors he considered when he hired her, even if he didn't fully admit that to himself at the time. But there was a big difference between noticing a pretty girl and what just went on, wasn't there? Or was he wrong?

He found himself pondering this last question during the next week. This made him a bit more distracted than usual, and may have been the reason that he did not follow up on his questions to his daughter about her recent activities when she arrived on Christmas Eve. Still, that didn't give Tricia the right to snap at him on Christmas afternoon, "Are you even listening to what I'm saying?" And it wasn't right that Sally took her side in the argument. After a few minutes, when neither Tricia nor Sally seemed very inclined to see his point of view, he finally said, "Well, it looks like you women just want to be on your own," and got his new scarf (from Tricia) and new gloves (from Sally) and left for a walk.

How was it that neither Tricia nor Sally understood the full import of the invitation to golf with Skip Smith at Dronin's house in Florida? Couldn't they see that this was an important first step in making some real contacts, contacts that could move him to a whole different level? Chances like this didn't come along very often. Pam certainly saw how important this was. Not only did she appreciate how important this opportunity was, she actively was trying to help him with her gift of golf lessons. That was so thoughtful. He should thank her again. He took out his cell phone and hit the speed dial button for her number.

"Bill?"

"Pam, Merry Christmas."

"Merry Christmas to you. Are you with your family?"

"I'm just taking a walk on my own. I wanted to thank you again for your really thoughtful gift."

"My pleasure. And thank you for the necklace. I'm wearing it now."

"Well, that's about it. Merry Christmas."

"And to you, Bill. I think this is going to be a really good year for CROSS."

"I hope so. Have a nice time with your sister."

"And you give my best to your family. Bye now."

"Bye."

He kept himself from calling Pamela again during the rest of the week, but he couldn't keep himself from thinking about her. He was more careful, however, about seeming to be engaged with his daughter over the rest of her stay with them, and also about being attentive to Sally during the rest of the holiday week. But he was looking forward to getting back to work.

He got into work early on January 2 and was at his desk when Pamela walked in. He immediately got up and went to her to welcome her back. As he drew closer, he saw she was wearing the necklace he gave her.

"Happy New Year" he said.

"Happy New Year to you Bill," She opened her arms to hug him.

This hug, like their last one, lasted a few beats longer than either of them had planned. And then, suddenly and without planning, but also without a good deal of surprise, they were kissing.

"I've wanted this for so long," Pamela finally said.

"Me, too. You understand me, you know where I'm going, and I want you to come with me."

Pamela pulled away a bit and looked him directly in his eyes. "Bill, won't this look bad for CROSS? What about our reputation, now that we're just now getting famous for our teenage abstinence work?"

"Pam, abstinence is for kids."

Chapter 35

Pamela Winship was nothing if not practical. She also had an ability to quickly size up a situation and determine what course of action to take. These attributes, along with her strawberry blonde hair, high cheekbones, and long legs, all helped her move from a small town in West Virginia through a series of jobs to her current position as assistant to the director of CROSS. And now, with an increase in the prospects of the director of CROSS, it could very well be that there was a corresponding increase in Pamela's prospects as well.

This is not to say that she didn't have real feelings for Bill Crocker. He was cute, in his own way, with a small cleft in his chin, bright blue eyes, and a mop of salt-and-pepper hair. But Pamela was always able to look beyond the physical. Bill was the kind of man that Pamela admired, one who acted when he saw an opportunity. The younger men with whom she had been involved had just promise, not accomplishment. Bill had accomplishment, and, especially now, the promise for even more.

She saw what had been happening at CROSS, and how things had changed. Up until recently, she thought things did not look too promising. In fact, she had started to look at the Help Wanted section of the *Washington Post* on Sundays in September, and had even taken a few furtive glances at job postings on the Internet during work in October. But, since then, things at CROSS were turning around. That teenage abstinence paper had gotten a lot of attention. It was clear that CROSS was moving up in the world. That meant that Bill Crocker was moving up in the world. And that might mean that Pamela Winship was moving up in the world, if she was smart about it. She had the ability to be smart about things like this. She knew that there was certainly precedence for men to move on as they moved up.

Bill could be convinced to move on, Pamela was sure of that. He had told her, with increasing frequency as their affair continued throughout January and into February, how she understood him in a way his wife did not. He told her that she had what it took to be a successful partner to him as he entered a whole new world of prestige and power. He told her that he and Sally had pretty much stopped being intimate.

She liked what Bill told her, but she was too smart to believe everything she was told. Not that he wasn't sincere. He probably meant every word of what he said, at least when he said it. But she knew that reality has a way of ruining the best intentions. She would just have to be a bit patient and very watchful.

Pamela had directed her watchfulness toward Bill and, to the extent that she could, toward Dronin. But in early February, she found a different, wholly unexpected source of concern. That boy, Greg Shankle, kept stopping by wanting to speak with Bill. Up until now, Greg had exhibited the standard sexual anxiety mixed with a bit of religious guilt that she saw in so many boys when she was younger. But Greg's current anxiety was different and hard for her to read. Greg seemed very anxious to talk with Bill and kept stopping back while Bill was in Florida. She told him that he was away, that he would be back on Monday, and "No, it would not be a good idea to phone him while he was meeting with Mr. Dronin." Frankly, Greg was becoming something of a pest.

Greg was really a pest the day Bill got back. She had followed Bill into his office when he first arrived. After hugging and kissing a bit, and some preliminary discussion during which each proclaimed to miss the other, Bill got down to business. He told her how well it had gone with Dronin and Skip Smith. They were both impressed by the fine work that CROSS was doing, and both, independently, had mentioned to Crocker that they saw a bright future ahead for him. But just as he was about to discuss some of the details of this bright future, there was a knock at the door.

Bill and Pam jumped apart, smoothing their clothes. Pam was impressed by how quickly Bill changed the tone of his voice to a professionally correct one. "Yes?" he called out. Greg entered.

"Hello, Dr. Crocker, Ms. Winship. Dr. Crocker, can I talk with you for a few moments?"

"Sure, Greg, what is it son?"

"Maybe we can talk alone?" Greg said, looking down at the floor.

Pam said that she had work to do anyway. She glanced back at Bill and winked as she softly closed the office door behind her.

Greg and Bill were in the office for quite a while. She heard some shouts but couldn't make out what they were saying. Eventually, the door opened and Greg left. He looked shaken up. Pam, a bit alarmed, walked right into Bill's office. Bill was staring out the window. He swung around in his chair when he heard her close the door behind her. She couldn't help but compare the lack of color in his face to the landscape she saw through the window, one in which the winter had drained the color from the hills in the distance.

"Bill, what is it?"

"Pam, 'Something for Nothing' is wrong."

"What?"

"Shankle found some kind of error in Fox's program."

"That bastard!"

"Pam, I don't think Fox was intentionally trying to fool anyone."

"I meant Greg! Why couldn't that twerp leave well enough alone!"

"Greg claims that abstinence programs actually increase pregnancy rates."

"How could that be?"

Bill answered sharply, "How should I know? Do I look like some wonky economist to you?" Bill's flash of anger surprised Pam and seemed to surprise him as well.

"Pam, I'm sorry," he continued. "I didn't mean anything by that. But this can be a disaster for us. And do you want to know what's even worse? Greg claims to have found that sex ed courses lower pregnancy rates. Dronin's not going to go for that, and Skip Smith sure as hell doesn't want CROSS to be saying that the administration is wrong about both abstinence programs and sex education."

"Well, we just have to make sure that Greg doesn't tell anyone about this."

"Greg already told Fox about this."

"Look, this is not rocket science. We tell both Greg and Fox that they are not to mention this to anyone."

"But Greg's all worked up about this. I'm not sure we can stop him from blabbing about this. He says it's the moral thing to do, since these results affect people's lives. He kept pointing to that damn *WWJA?* bracelet he wears."

"Greg might be a little less moral if his blabbing gets him kicked out of SAVE."

"That won't work. Greg probably would like to play the martyr."

Pam thought for a moment. Then she said, "Greg would not be expelled for his beliefs, he would be expelled because he falsified his time sheets."

Bill was surprised. "He did?"

"He very well might have. We would have to check," Pam answered, raising an eyebrow.

Bill finally got it. "But what about Fox?"

"Could we tell his employer he lied?"

Bill brightened. "No, it's better than that. Fox is looking for a job now. It would be a shame if the schools where he was applying learned that he had misled us by falsifying his results."

Pam's faith in Bill was being restored. Maybe there was hope for him yet. And for her.

Chapter 36

"Hello?"

"Hi, David. It's Greg."

"Greg, hi, how are you?"

"Okay. Well, actually, not so good."

"What's wrong? You sound worried."

"I spoke with Dr. Crocker yesterday and told him about our new results. He got pretty angry."

"I can't say that I'm surprised."

"Crocker said that if I told anybody about those results he would have me kicked out of SAVE."

"He can't do that."

"He can, and he said he would. He also said that there were some problems with the time sheets I turned in, and they would be considering whether that meant I had stolen money from CROSS."

"That sounds like a crock of shit! They're just trying to scare you."

"I may have messed up some of the time sheets. I thought they had a rule about studying during working hours, but Crocker told me that was wrong, that should have been on my own time. He said he would be willing to overlook it, but only if I was a 'team player.'"

"Well, I don't have to be a team player. They can't do anything to me. Remember how I told you I would take the heat? I can do that. Just tell Crocker that it was my fault."

"David, Crocker already thinks it's your fault, too. And he said that if I tried to get you to help me out, he would tell all the schools where you had fly- outs that you purposefully falsified the data to try to get a *CROSS Currents* working paper to help you get a job."

"You know that I didn't do that!"

"I know, David, but Dr. Crocker said that he was sure you must have messed with the data, and he was willing to tell the schools that."

"How would he know where I have fly-outs anyway?"

"I guess I told him."

"You told him! Greg, why would you do that?"

"I didn't know that he was going to use it against you, I swear to the Lord I didn't. At first, Crocker told me he wanted to protect you, and he needed to know who to contact if all of this started to fall apart. But then, after he threatened to expel me, he told me what he would do to you if you tried to tell people about the results."

"Look, let me think about this for a while. I'll call you back in an hour."

"Okay, David, bye."

"Bye."

"Hello."

"Hi, it's David. Greg, I've been thinking, and we should just go along with Crocker."

"What do you mean?"

"Let's just not say anything to anybody about your new results, or about the original results in 'Something for Nothing' being wrong. I can just deflect questions about 'Something for Nothing' when I'm on fly-outs. When I was visiting Brunsfield, I found out how badly people react to learning that the results were wrong, so I just won't say anything."

"You said that you were going to tell people to preempt the criticism."

"Well, I'm not sure that works so well. It's better if I just ignore it. And it would be better if you just ignored it, too, Greg."

"What are you saying, I should just keep on with my work at CROSS like nothing happened?"

"That's exactly what I'm saying. Look, in a couple of years, once I have a job and once you've completed your PhD, Crocker won't have any hold over us. We can work on the paper then. Until then, just forget about all of this."

"But we know the results are wrong."

"Greg, who cares?"

"I care, and you should, too. Besides, if we know that abstinence programs are harmful and sex education is helpful, we have a moral duty to let people know."

"Moral duty! This is just research; it's a game. We're a couple of two-bit economists and no one cares what we write. We could spend months and months on this and then get some cranky journal editor who decides to not publish the article because he's never heard of us before. Even if it does get published, do you think any more than five people would ever read it? You're the statistician, what are the odds that any of those five people would affect policy? Greg, the only moral duty we have is to ourselves—to play this game well and try to get a chance even though the game is rigged."

"David, don't get angry, I'm sorry. You're right, we can just wait on this."

"I'm sorry I yelled. It's just so frustrating. Look, let's just stay quiet about all of this for a while. No one is paying any attention to 'Something for Nothing' now anyway. We have time. There's no need to be hasty."

"Okay. Neither of us will say anything. You take care now, and good luck on your fly-outs."

"Thanks, Greg. Good luck at CROSS. Just keep your head down, and you'll be all right. Bye."

"Bye, and God bless."

"Whatever."

Chapter 37

There's a geography of classroom seating familiar to anyone who has attended a medium-sized college course. No men sit in the front row, and almost no women sit in the back row. The women who sit in the front row are those who take neat, well-organized notes, answer questions, and do not challenge the professor's opinion. The men who sit in the back row may take notes, or they may just be doodling. They never voluntarily answer questions. The second and third rows are filled with students who are committed to the class but are also concerned about not appearing too earnest. The next-to-last rows include men and women who are committed to the truth, as they see it, and are more than willing to challenge false assertions, bourgeois attitudes, and incomplete logic. Students sitting within these extremes try to pay attention most of the time, respond to questions if they're pretty sure of the answer, and keep their doubts about the relevance of the material to themselves.

Jenny Lake had been a front-row student in the Economics of Social Issues course that David taught in the fall semester. She began the spring semester as the only woman sitting in the last row of the classroom in his Environmental Economics course. David took note of her relocation on the first day of class. He knew that the last row was, for her, a type of exile, one for which he shared some blame. But he took it as a good sign that she showed up to the class at all.

The last row was not a natural habitat for Jenny, and, over the next two weeks of class, she slowly moved forward. She sat in the next-to-last row during the second meeting of the class, among those who were waiting for a chance to challenge the professor if he demonstrated insufficient sympathy to the plight of the Earth. She held this position for the third class, but by the end of the second week of classes, she was in the middle of the room. Like her neighbors there, she did not offer comments unbidden but would answer the few questions that David posed to her with the precision of a front-row student.

Jenny's continued willingness to take David's course, however, was not matched by an inclination to return to his office to discuss her thesis. David was concerned about this. Her work had shown such promise, and he hated to think that one stupid act could have derailed her project. But he felt uneasy about asking her to come by his office, even if he were to take the extreme step of removing its door from its hinges, something he briefly considered. No, he had to bide his time. And, like a naturalist watching a wary animal, he tried not to spook her as he observed Jenny moving, row by row, toward her accustomed territory, in the front of the room, as the semester progressed.

Finally, in the middle of February, Jenny walked into the class-room animated and laughing, just as she did in the fall semester. She was talking with Stephen Conley, who David knew from last semester's Social Issues. Stephen was a senior, an economics major, and a good student, and he was handsome in a tousled sort of way.

Stephen and Jenny took seats next to each other in the third row, the first time, in David's memory, that they had sat together. They continued to chat quietly, leaning their heads together, as David began lecturing. He looked at them and raised his eyebrows, and they stopped talking, but they didn't stop smiling. They passed notes back and forth during class, and, at the end of the hour, left together, their shoulders brushing. David couldn't be happier for the new couple. Or more relieved.

The next day, a Wednesday, Jenny stopped by during his office hours and knocked on the open door.

"Hi, Professor Fox. Do you have some time now?"

"Sure, Jenny, come on in."

He saw her glance toward his desk, but the shot glass had long since been removed.

"Well, I know that it's been a while, but I have been working on my thesis. I just didn't have a chance to come by during your office hours to talk to you about it."

"That's okay, I know how it is. I'm glad you're making progress. Will you have something to show me soon, like a rough draft or an outline?"

"Hopefully I'll have a rough draft for you in another couple of weeks. I've done the first round of regressions, along the lines of what you suggested, and the results look pretty good."

"Great, that's wonderful. You still have plenty of time, but you should keep working on it steadily. Don't leave it all until a week before it's due."

"You know me. I wouldn't do that."

"I know, but I have to say that. It's part of my job."

"Okay, well, just wanted to check in. See you in class."

David could have let it end there, but he didn't.

"I'm really sorry, you know."

She looked at him and then at the floor.

"Me, too. I feel like it was my fault."

"No, it wasn't. You shouldn't think that at all. If it was anyone's fault, it was mine."

"I guess we can just forget about it, huh?"

"That would probably be best. But don't forget about your thesis, okay?"

"I won't. I've gotta go now. I'm meeting Steve at the campus center."

"See you in class tomorrow."

"Bye, Professor."

"Bye, Jenny."

As he watched her walk away, he admired her nice ass once again. He was very thankful that Stephen Conley had apparently also taken notice of it.

Subject: Article on CROSS
Date: 2/12/2008, 1:13 PM
To: William Crocker <william.crocker@cross.org>
From: Mason Freeman <mfreeman@libertyreview.com>

Dear Dr. Crocker,

My name is Mason Freeman, and I'm a staff writer at the *Liberty Review*. I believe that my editor, John Clark, has been in touch with you about a story we would like to do on Christian think tanks. We have decided to focus our story on CROSS, and especially on your success in promoting abstinence programs through the publication of "Something for Nothing."

I will be in touch with you by phone in the next day or two in order to set up a visit to CROSS. The *Liberty Review* will also be hiring a photographer who will be contacting you.

I look forward to speaking with you soon and to meeting you in person in a couple of weeks.

Sincerely,
Mason
Mason Freeman
The Liberty Review

Spring Break

Chapter 38

Locals refer to five seasons in upstate New York: spring, summer, fall, winter, and mud. Kester College's one-week vacation in mid-March is called "spring break." "Mud break" would more accurately reflect regional conditions at the time.

"Mud" was also a pretty good description of David's emotional state by the beginning of March. He had phoned Angie a couple of times in February. Their conversations were cordial enough. She asked about his job search, and he tried to sound positive. He made a point of asking about her job, and of sounding encouraging about her prospects at KnitWare. He told her he had been swimming; she told him she was traveling and getting out of shape. They each had opinions about when spring would arrive. But he did not feel comfortable carrying the conversation beyond jobs, exercise, and the weather. He listened for a clue that suggested that Angie was looking for an offer to get together again. Maybe it was there, maybe not. Giovanna's closing words during his call in January, "I'm sorry," clearly made it harder for him to hear something encouraging. It seemed too risky to extend an offer and receive a final rejection that would conclusively shut the door.

"Mud" was also a better description of David's professional prospects in March than "spring." He felt mired rather than ready to spring ahead. He had completed the rest of his fly-outs by the end of February. In keeping with his agreement with Greg, and learning from his experience at Brunsfield, he downplayed "Something for Nothing" and his ten minutes of fame at all the other colleges he visited. He never directly lied about the results in his published *CROSS Currents* working paper. Instead, when asked about his research on abstinence programs, he would always offer some vague remarks about the context provided by the wider literature, robustness, and confidence intervals. He became adept at segueing from this topic into a discussion of his dissertation research on the effect of incentives on environmental programs. In almost all cases, the interviewers were too polite to break into his spiel, or to ask him to return to the topic of abstinence, once he had moved on to the subject of the environment.

The exception was at Grindle. Mitchell Fredricks, the chair of the Grindle search committee, wanted to pick up their discussion where they had left off in Boston. He was truly fascinated by the notoriety he believed David had acquired through his interview with Alan Glidden on *Talk Right*. David did his best to parry Mitchell's questions during the day. But finally, at dinner that evening, it all became too much; the constant harping about talk radio, his rapidly waning respect for Mitchell, the fatigue from the long day, and the cumulative tension of diverting discussion about "Something for Nothing" during a month of fly-outs. He didn't want to teach at Grindle, and he certainly didn't want to have an office down the hall from Mitchell Fredricks. He finally blurted out, "Mitchell, I really don't want to discuss *Talk Right*, okay? I don't know Alan Glidden. I'll never be on that show again. Frankly, it was an embarrassment. So can we just drop it?" The dinner conversation deflated after that. David figured he would never be on the campus of Grindle again.

Soon after this, David learned that he would also never be on the campus of Brunsfield again. Linda Goldman phoned him in late February to tell him that they had extended an offer to another candidate who had accepted almost immediately. Linda offered some kind words about her hopes for his opportunities at other schools and also let him know that he was their second choice.

The other fly-outs were largely unexceptional. Mitford College was a pleasant enough place in many ways, but the economists there were overly impressed with their own perceived accomplishments. The Mitford Economics Department was one of the hundred departments across the country that self-ranked in the top twenty-five. If the economics faculty at Mitford suffered from taking itself too seriously, those at Crest College were plagued by self-doubt. David wasn't a stranger to self-doubt; in fact, he found it a useful spur to work harder. The professors at Crest College, however, decided that if they couldn't measure up, why try? There were a surprising number of questions at Crest about his willingness to play on the Economics Department intramural teams—flag football in the fall, basketball in the winter, and softball in the spring. He felt as if he should have been showing a sports highlights film rather than discussing a research paper for his presentation there.

By March, the two remaining hopes were Sewall College and Kester. The trip at the end of February to central Maine to interview at Sewall went well, or at least well enough. There was some interest in "Something for Nothing," but he was able to divert conversation from that to his real research interests. The faculty at Sewall also seemed nice enough, serious about teaching, reasonably active in research, and, from what he could glean, interested in having lives outside their jobs. When he left Sewall, Professor Salant, the chair of the search committee, said, "Thanks for coming, David, we'll be in touch." Those last few words remained his best hope for a successful job search as March began.

His best hope, but not his last one. Like all the places that he had visited, the Kester Economics Department had its candidates come through in February. Kester had an internal candidate also, and the decision was made to have David present his talk at the end of the regular process, in March. Murray Stern came by his office and told him of this decision in early February. Murray seemed to hint that this gave him a slight advantage, one the economists at Kester were pleased to afford him since they had all heard good things about his teaching during the fall semester. David appreciated this, but it was still difficult to bear continual witness to a search in which he was a candidate. Avoiding all the other candidates' job talks didn't mean avoiding the weekly seminar posters, or avoiding concern about how his Kester colleagues liked Peter Berlton (PhD Stanford University, "The Market for Marriage and the Bazaar for Divorce"), Jay Chadha (PhD UC Berkeley, "How Now Brown Cow?: What the Genetically Modified Food Controversy Means for U.S. Agriculture"), or Cynthia Wellinsky (PhD University of Pennsylvania, "Discrimination in Hiring by TV News Organizations and the Economic Returns to Good Hair").

Finally, at the end of February, Murray stopped by his office to tell him that the committee would like him to present a research seminar in two weeks' time, during the week before spring break. Like all the other candidates, he would have the opportunity during that seminar to show his potential for conducting successful research.

"I suppose you would want to present your 'Something for Nothing' paper."

He did not welcome this suggestion. It did show, however, that Jeff had kept his promise about not mentioning the problems with that paper to anyone, not even to Murray who, as far as David could tell, was the senior faculty member with whom Jeff felt closest.

"Actually, Murray, my future research will probably be in the area of environmental economics, so I'd like to present my dissertation chapter instead."

"It's your choice, David, but you should know that the dean of the college likes to sit in on these talks. He was interested in the publicity that Kester could get if this paper continued to attract attention. The dean doesn't have a vote on the decision of which candidate we choose, but he does have a lot of influence, especially with Wellingham."

"Thanks, Murray. I'll think about it, but I'll probably still go with the dissertation chapter. I'll let you know in a few days."

"Okay, David. Good luck."

He thought he would wait a few days to inform Murray about a decision that he had already made, in order to give the impression that he had seriously considered the suggestion. As it turned out, however, the dean of the college was not the only one who wanted to hear a seminar on "Something for Nothing."

Chapter 39

"Tell me about the Center to Research Opportunities for a Spiritual Society."

Crocker leaned back in his chair slightly and put his hands on his desk. He wanted to exude a sense of gravitas to Mason Freeman, but he didn't want to come across as pompous. The right pose would be one where he and Freeman conversed as equals, man-to-man, or, even better yet, thinking-man-of-the-right-to-thinking-man-of-the-right. And also friend-to-friend. He wanted Freeman to feel that they were friends, even though they had just met that morning.

His first impression of Freeman worried him a little. In his rumpled sports coat, corduroy pants, and casual suede shoes, he seemed a bit disheveled, at least compared to the people of power that Crocker was used to dealing with. Of course, Freeman's power came from his writing, not from his personal presence. And Freeman did seem to have power, at least as far as Crocker could tell. The *Liberty Review* was one of the flagship publications of the libertarian wing of the right, and Freeman was a regular contributor. Pam had gathered back issues of the magazine and copied articles by Freeman. He carefully read Freeman's recent work on efforts by the government to illegally acquire privately held land in the western United States using eminent domain ("What's Mine Is Theirs"), the negative incentive effects of high marginal tax rates ("Rich *and* Lazy?"), and the threats to the Second Amendment ("A Shotgun Approach"). But Freeman had also written articles with a libertarian cant that others on the right might take exception to, including one questioning the mandatory teaching of creationism ("Out of the Slime") and another on the use of medical marijuana ("Weed Eradication?").

Pam had carefully planned Freeman's visit. A private limousine had been hired to transport him from Washington the previous evening. Freeman's day at CROSS began with a private breakfast with Crocker, followed by a tour of the CROSS offices. He then took Freeman on a tour of the SAVE campus. As Pam suggested, he used this time to try to get a sense of the angle Freeman wanted to take in his article, but Freeman skillfully turned these questions to him into his own inquiries about Crocker and his goals—questions that Crocker, even while understanding what was going on, found himself answering at length.

Now, back at his office, he could once again take command of the situation and direct the conversation. Freeman had tossed him a softball. He had every intention of hitting it out of the park.

"Mason, there's a need, a real need, to back up the political aspirations of people of faith with hard analytical research. Here at CROSS, we produce research that can be used to bolster arguments in favor of the kind of faith-based initiatives that all of us would like to see enacted in order to make ours a more godly nation."

"Do you yourself participate in conducting that research, Bill? I know you have a PhD in economics."

"I do, yes, and I would love to have the opportunity to get down and dirty with the data, but the demands of running this think tank just take too much time. No, my role is one where I guide and oversee the work that's done here. I try to give direction, and focus, and to maintain a wider perspective that's so important for a think tank like CROSS to be successful."

"So who does most of the actual research? Do you at CROSS work closely with the people at SAVE?"

"SAVE is a relatively new program, and we won't have it fully online to contribute for a year or two now. But we do have some of the finest young people at SAVE working for us now. It's a mentoring process, if you will."

"I would like the opportunity to meet those people. Can you tell me some of their names?"

He hesitated, realizing that the more accurate word would have been "person" rather than "people," but then he quickly recovered.

"Almost all of the young people from SAVE that are working for us are out of town now, but we do have one of our SAVE students, in fact our star SAVE student, in the office today. His name is Greg Shankle."

"I'd like to have the chance to chat with him."

"I'll see if that can be arranged, but your limousine leaves at 3:00 today."

"Well, maybe I could follow up and just have a phone interview with Mr. Shankle."

Greg could be a loose cannon, but he would be more easily tethered in the presence of Crocker himself rather than off somewhere on the phone. "Mason, I'll ask Pam to have Greg come by." He picked up the phone and called Pam.

"That's great. Thanks for being so accommodating. Of course, since 'Something for Nothing' has been the thing that really put CROSS on the map, I'd like to speak with David Fox as well. Can you put him in touch with me?"

This was going to be trickier. Greg was easy to control; he was right there at CROSS where he could keep an eye on him. Who knows what Fox might say? He didn't like the idea of Mason and Fox together without a chaperone. Better to keep Fox out of this altogether.

"Fox is one of the young stars of our stable. In fact, this year he's been interviewing for some prestigious academic posts. He's on a pretty heavy travel schedule right now, so it might be hard to speak with him before your deadline."

"That's too bad. I don't think the article would have the same heft without interviewing Fox since we really want to get at the meat of the analysis. But maybe, instead of Fox, you could go through some of the details of the analysis with me."

"I would love to do that, I really would, but that wouldn't be fair to David now, would it? No, we wouldn't want to rob a young scholar of his chance to get this kind of coverage—why coverage like this could help make his career. I'll tell you what. Let me talk to Fox, and I will get you a meeting with him as soon as possible."

"Wonderful. I realize that arranging this might not be easy, so I'd be willing to travel to—where is it?—Kester College to interview Fox."

"Why, we could go together. That would be fun. I haven't seen David for a few months now and would love the chance to visit with him again. And you know what, if we travel together, why CROSS would be more than happy to pay your way."

There was a soft knock at the door. Pam opened the door and announced, "Greg Shankle is here to see you, Mr. Crocker."

"Thanks so much, Pam. Send him in."

Greg entered the office, looking nervous. He glanced at Crocker, and then at Freeman, and then back at Crocker again.

"Greg, good to see you, and thanks so much for coming by. This is Mr. Mason Freeman, a writer for the *Liberty Review*. Mr. Freeman wants to do a story on CROSS and on SAVE, and he would like the perspective of the young people around here. Could you take a few minutes to talk with us?"

"Sure, Dr. Crocker, I'd be happy to help out."

"Thank you, Greg. Why don't you just sit right there, and Mr. Mason can ask you a few questions."

He directed Greg to a seat on the couch, seating him such that Mason would have his back to Crocker, but Greg could see Crocker over Mason's shoulder. Greg wasn't dumb; he would quickly understand what Crocker had done, and why.

"Thank you for meeting with me on such short notice, Greg. Can I call you Greg?"

"Sure, Mr. Mason."

"How long have you been here?"

"This is my second year at SAVE, and I've been working for CROSS since the fall."

"How do you like it?" It was an innocent question, really just a filler, but Greg glanced at Crocker before he answered. He smiled at him and nodded slightly.

"This is a wonderful opportunity, it really is."

"What do you like about it?"

"I get a chance to work on research that I believe in." Unfortunately, there was a bit of an inflection to that statement, so it sounded a little like Greg had posed a question.

"What do you believe in?"

"I believe in God, sir," Greg answered. Freeman and Crocker both laughed.

"No, Greg, what research do you believe in?"

Greg thought for a moment. He wanted to be careful, but he also had a natural aversion to lying. "Sir, I love economics, I really do. It's fun for me, kind of like doing a game, er, I mean a puzzle. But it's more than that. It's a way to make a difference by showing people some truths about the world. I truly believe that, if people know the truth, they'll do the right thing. So, really, economics can help people do the right thing."

"That's wonderful. Those are very nice sentiments." said Freeman, who had taken out his pad for the first time and began taking notes. "What are some of the actual tasks that you do for CROSS?"

"I try to help Dr. Crocker by identifying research projects that could be helpful for us."

"Like 'Something for Nothing'?"

"Yeah, I was the one who found Professor Fox's paper."

Time to interject. "It's such a blessing to have talented young people like Greg to help me out in my search for good works."

"I'm sure it is, Bill," said Freeman over his shoulder. He continued, "Greg, just one more question, then I'll let you get back to your work. Have you read 'Something for Nothing'? What do you think about it?"

Greg paused for a minute and then answered, "I learned a lot."

Chapter 40

"Hello?"

A vaguely familiar woman's voice said, "Professor David Fox, please."

"This is Professor Fox."

"Please hold for a call from Bill Crocker."

In the few seconds before Crocker came on the line, he felt his heart sink. This call had been expected ever since Greg alerted him that some magazine writer had visited CROSS. In fact, a call from Crocker was anticipated ever since early January when Greg told him about the flaws in "Something for Nothing."

"David, Bill Crocker. It's good to speak with you again."

He was surprised at the pleasant tone of Crocker's voice, given what he expected this call to be about. He tried to match that tone in his own response.

"How are you, Bill?"

"I'm fine, David, just fine. I've got some exciting news for you. It looks like you're going to get some more good publicity. The *Liberty Review* wants to do a cover story on CROSS, one that will prominently feature your research. This can help you out on your job search, I'm sure."

He was not expecting this. Greg had told Crocker about the mistakes in the original paper and also about the new results. The editors of the *Liberty Review*, which David thought was probably a mouthpiece for the extreme right, wouldn't be interested in the failure of abstinence programs and the efficacy of sex education, would they?

"Bill, are you sure that the *Liberty Review* wants to publicize the results we have?"

"Oh, I'm very sure of that, David."

"Have you spoken to Greg recently about some of the issues that we have with the results in 'Something for Nothing'?"

"Greg has gotten worked up about a few things, but I wouldn't put too much credence in that. There will always be nit-picking about research, won't there."

"Bill, I don't think this is just an issue of picking some nits; it seems like the results in the original paper are completely wrong."

"Now David, I know that you're just starting out in this business, but you have to have more confidence in yourself."

Maybe Crocker just didn't understand Greg's points. Maybe he was unwilling to believe that a grad student at SAVE would have found legitimate and lethal flaws in the work of a professor who had graduated from Columbia. But Greg was right, no doubt about it. Could it be that Greg, upset at finding the mistake, had overreacted and misinterpreted Crocker's response?

"Bill," he said, hoping to convey their common interest, "we really need to consider Greg's criticisms seriously. I carefully looked through what he did, and he was right; there was a mistake with the original paper. Greg's new findings about sex ed classes, as far as I can tell, are also correct. So maybe we should just try put off this interview with the *Liberty Review* for a while until we can clear things up."

There was more of an edge to Crocker's voice when he responded. "That isn't really an option, David. The article is scheduled to appear soon, and you know how deadlines work in publishing."

"Well maybe the article can just be about CROSS, and avoid mentioning 'Something for Nothing.'"

"No, David, the writer was quite adamant. He wants to feature you and your work in this article as well."

He was getting concerned, more by the shifting tone in Crocker's voice than by the words themselves.

"Bill, I'm just not comfortable with that."

"Well, son, you better start getting comfortable, and soon. This story is going to get written, it's going to talk about your work, and you're going to go along."

"I really would rather not do that."

"I don't care what you want. You want a job, don't you? How do you think colleges are going to respond when they find out that you screwed with the data just to get your work published by CROSS?"

"You know that's not what happened!"

"Do I?" Crocker asked coolly. "How would I know that?"

"Greg found a programming error. It was an honest mistake."

"I'll remind you, David, that your friend Greg works for me and wants to get a degree from my institution. I think Greg can be persuaded to see things my way."

Son of a bitch, Greg was right.

"You have a lot of chutzpah."

"Around here we would say 'I have balls,' and I do, so I would advise you not to fuck with me. We can get through this together, and we'll all be the better off for it."

"All right, I won't say anything about the *Liberty Review* article when it gets published."

"I'm afraid I need more than your silence, I need your help. It seems that Mr. Mason Freeman, the writer of this article, wants to interview you and is willing to come to Kester for a visit. I myself have never had an opportunity to visit Kester, so I offered to accompany Freeman on his visit. That way, I can meet you face-to-face as well. We'll be visiting you next Wednesday. I hope you're free."

"I'm giving my job talk at Kester next Wednesday."

The line was silent for a few seconds before Crocker said, "That's even better. These job talks are open to the public, aren't they? I'm sure that the administration up at Kester would be very pleased to have the media attend your talk. It's wonderful when scholarly work can have an impact on the public debate. I'll have my secretary notify your department chairman, and even the president's office, that Mr. Mason and I will be attending your lecture for the purposes of writing an article that will feature not only you and your work but Kester College as well."

"Bill, that's not a good idea."

"On the contrary, David, I think this is a very good idea, maybe one of the best I've had in a while."

"But this is my career!"

"Mine, too, young man, and both of us can profit from this."

"Don't do this to me, please."

"David, everything will be fine. That is, if you do a good job. And I'm sure a bright young man like you can do a good job when so much is on the line. On the other hand, if the seminar doesn't go well, I may discover problems with the data that you failed to tell me about. I'm sure the Kester economics faculty would be very interested in that when they consider whether to offer you a job."

"You wouldn't do that."

"Try me." With that, the line went dead.

David slammed the receiver, swore loudly, and then sank into his office chair.

Chapter 41

David would have paced around his office, but the space was far too small. He had to get out. So, without packing his briefcase or turning off his computer, he grabbed his jacket, left his office, exited Central Hall, and walked off the campus of Kester College and onto the streets of Knittersville.

The days were getting longer and, even though it was 4:30, the sun was warm. As he began to walk, he thought about Crocker, "Something for Nothing," and his upcoming presentation next week. But, as the shadows got longer and the air cooled, he found himself focusing more on his surroundings. Mud season was just beginning in upstate New York. The large snow drifts of February had become much smaller, pockmarked and dirty. Sidewalks narrowed by snow had widened. Patches of grass poked through in the middle of lawns. The smell of wet dirt was in the air.

This was not what comes to mind when someone says "college town." But, like it or not, Knittersville was a college town. Or, rather, it was a town that had a college in it.

It also had neighborhoods that were far from the college, neighborhoods that were neither especially nice nor especially bad, just average places to live. He walked through these neighborhoods, many for the first time, and looked at the one- and two-story houses. Lights in the houses turned on as the daylight began to fade. Inside were people who had just come home from their jobs, who were getting ready for dinner, who were talking with each other about what they had done that day.

It began to get cold. He had wandered into a familiar neighborhood. He walked down the block, looking in the lit windows of the houses, and, at the end of the block, turned and retraced his steps. He stopped in front of a two-family house, and, after hesitating for only a few seconds, walked up its steps and rang the doorbell.

"Hello, Giovanna. Is Angie here?"

He tried to read her face, which registered surprise, but what else? "Wait here, David."

Giovanna closed the door behind her and disappeared into the house. He turned and looked at the grass that showed through the snow in the small front lawn. He heard the door open and turned around.

Angie had come onto the porch and closed the door behind her. David had not seen her since their last dinner together in December. She pulled her blue cardigan around her, hunched her shoulders, and tucked her arms across her chest. David remembered a time when she wore that cardigan, and nothing else, in his bed when he brought her a cup of coffee one morning. She tucked a loose strand of hair behind her ear and looked at him for a moment, tilting her head slightly. How had he ever let her get away?

"David, what are you doing here?"

"Hi, Angie."

"Hi, David. What are you doing here?"

"I thought it'd be nice to see you."

"Why didn't you call first?"

"I didn't plan this out. I was just walking around and happened to be here."

"You were just walking around near my house? By coincidence?"

"Actually, I was just walking around all over Knittersville. It's not that much of a coincidence that I'd eventually be near your house. It's not that big a town."

Angie laughed. He had not heard that laugh in a very long time, longer than the time since he had last seen her. He remembered how much he liked her laugh.

"Okay, Angie, it wasn't really a coincidence, but I did spend a long time walking around before I got here."

"Are you alright?"

"Yes, well, more or less."

"Are you sick?"

"No, nothing like that."

"Did you get another job?"

"No, not yet. Maybe not at all. I don't know. It's not over yet. But it's not really looking very good."

"What happened?"

He didn't want to launch into the story, not now when this was the first he had seen her since last year. He protested that she'd be bored by it all, but she insisted. He told her about Greg, and about the programming mistake he'd made and how the people at Brunsfield had reacted to that, and how all the other interviews after that felt flat, and how he had only two schools left, one of them being Kester, and how Crocker had threatened him, and how he didn't know what to do.

"I'm sorry about this, David."

"Yeah, me, too."

"You know, after all is said and done, it's just a job."

"What?"

"It's just a job."

"Angie, I've spent the last six years working toward this. I went to grad school, I haven't had any money, I lived like a friggin' monk, and now it's about to blow up in my face."

She began to get angry. "David, it's just a job. There should be more to your life than your job. When are you going to learn that?"

She had a knack for asking good questions.

"Angie, you're right. I'm sorry, I really am."

"Me, too."

They stood there for a while in silence.

"Why didn't you come by before this, or ask me out again?" she finally asked in a soft voice.

"I wanted to, I really did. But I didn't think you wanted to see me. It was nice talking to you on the phone, but I felt like you were holding back. I guess I was afraid to ask."

"Yeah, I guess I was a little afraid that you would ask."

"Is there someone else?"

"No. Well, not really. There was someone, sort of, for a while, but there isn't anymore. Anyone else for you?"

"No, Angie, no one else. No one at all."

They stood in silence. It was dark, and by now all the street-lights were on. He looked at the planks on the front porch. Some of them would need to be replaced this spring. He looked up at Angie. She had been staring at him. Their eyes met. She reached out and took hold of the sleeve of his coat. He took his hand out of his pocket and held her hand.

"It's getting cold," she said.

"I know. I should get going."

"Did you eat?"

"No, I'll get something on my way home."

"Why don't you stay for dinner. My mom cooked."

"I don't want to put you out."

"My mom would like it. She asks about you."

"Really?"

"Yeah, really. And I'd like it, too."

"Really?"

"Yeah, really."

"Well, okay, thanks, thanks a lot. That would be nice."

Without letting go of his hand, she turned and opened the door. Hand in hand, they went into the house where it was warm and light.

Chapter 42

"Professor Geoffrey Wellingham, please."

"This is Professor Wellingham."

"Please hold for a call from Dr. William Crocker, director of CROSS."

Professor Wellingham tried to recall if he had ever met Dr. William Crocker, or if he had heard of CROSS before. He could not answer either of these two questions in the few seconds available to him. But he did immediately realize that a call initiated by someone's secretary was a call worth taking.

"Professor Wellingham, this is Bill Crocker."

"Dr. Crocker, good to speak with you. What can I do for you today?"

"Well, Professor, there isn't much that you can do for me today, but there is something that you can do for me next week, and something that I can do for you at that time."

"Yes?"

"Professor Wellingham, I'm the Director of CROSS, an economic think tank in Virginia. As you know, we have published the work of your Professor Fox."

"That's it," thought Wellingham to himself, "Fox published that working paper with them and then got interviewed on TV or radio or something."

"Ah, Fox, one of our young turks. Yes, we are very fond of him here."

"As are we, Professor, as are we. We think that Professor Fox has a great future in front of him. In fact, that's why I'm calling you today. You know the *Liberty Review*, I'm sure."

Wellingham did not. "Of course."

"The *Liberty Review* wants to do a story on Fox, and on the research that he has published with us. As I understand it, Professor Fox is giving a public lecture next Wednesday."

Wellingham quickly consulted the calendar on his desk. "Actually, it's his job market seminar."

"Which, of course, is open to the public."

"Of course."

"Well, the head features writer for the *Liberty Review* would like to cover this public lecture, and, as a courtesy, I'll be accompanying him on his trip to Kester College. Kester would figure prominently in the forthcoming article, I'm sure."

Wellingham had been chair of economics for quite a few years and, therefore, quickly understood what this opportunity could mean for his efforts to secure scarce college resources for his department.

"That would be wonderful, Dr. Crocker."

Crocker continued, "I'm sure that a lecture by Professor Fox, someone who has been getting a lot of media attention lately, would generate a lot of interest among other faculty and students."

Wellingham thought of the last job market seminar he attended, a week or so ago, by a young woman named Wollins or something. Pretty girl. Something about TV news. Too bad there were only five people in the room at the time.

"These seminars are often well attended."

"That's good. It will look better for Kester if there is an appropriate level of appreciation of your up-and-coming faculty."

Wellingham cradled the receiver on his shoulder as he got a pen and wrote a note to himself to tell Peggy to make better flyers to announce Fox's talk and to distribute them more widely. "We expect quite a big crowd. In fact, we have scheduled the largest room here in Central Hall for Professor Fox's lecture."

"Wonderful, I'm sure that will help make a good impression on our friend from the *Liberty Review*. So then, until next week."

"Very nice speaking with you, Dr. Crocker."

"And with you, Professor Wellingham. Good day."

"Good day."

Wellingham hung up the phone, and immediately rose from his desk and went down the hall to Peggy Albert's office.

"Peggy, good news. We are hosting the media next week. A writer from a national magazine will be reporting on David Fox's lecture."

Peggy seemed less thrilled than he would have expected.

"Professor Wellingham, David's lecture is his job talk."

"Yes, I know that."

"Is it fair to invite the media to someone's job talk? I mean, David will be nervous enough since so much rides on this."

He had not thought of that. Still, Fox was already well known by the people in the department, wasn't he? Wellingham knew, from his own experience in hiring over the years, that once a candidate made an impression there was not much that would alter it, certainly not one lecture on some obscure academic topic. And this was such a good opportunity for the economics department.

The dean of the college will be there. Wouldn't it be much better for him to see a crowd of people as well as a representative from a national publication rather than a few bored-looking professors, like what happened at Miss Wollins's talk last week? Even if the heightened attention wasn't the optimal thing for Fox, one had to weigh competing interests in a situation like this. Besides, Fox might appreciate the attention, and he might even thrive if given the chance to speak in front of a substantial audience.

"Peggy, if anything, this gives Fox an advantage. Which is fine with me, because I like the fellow. No, it's settled. Please book Room 1 for the talk. Also, I'll need you to make up some new posters. Use the color printer, and make them more noticeable than the ones we have now. Make sure that the new posters get distributed to other departments and in the student union. Oh, and arrange for a reception with some food and drink afterward. Be sure to mention the reception on the new poster."

Peggy agreed, with what seemed to him like some measure of reluctance. Frankly, he was a bit surprised by her attitude since she never seemed to mind taking on extra work in the past. Perhaps because he had not given her much lead time and had just sprung this on her. Never mind, she'll come around. Long experience had shown him that Peggy truly did have the best interest of the department at heart.

Kester College
Economics Department
is pleased to announce a seminar entitled

Something for Nothing

by

Professor David Fox

What is the effect of teenage abstinence programs?

Professor Fox's provocative paper, which has garnered national attention, provides some surprising results.

This seminar will be held
on
Wednesday, March 15, 2008
at
3:00–4:30
in
Room 1, Central Hall.
All members of the Kester community,
and all interested visitors, are invited to attend.

A reception will follow the seminar.

Chapter 43

Jeff White answered the knock on his office door. "Yes?"

It was David. "Hi, Jeff, do you want to get lunch today?"

"Sure, where do you want to go?"

"The cafeteria would be fine."

"I thought you were avoiding the cafeteria because you didn't want to see Giovanna."

"No, that's okay. I actually saw Giovanna yesterday."

"On a Sunday?"

"Yeah, I saw her when I went to pick up Angie."

Jeff leaned back in his chair and smiled. "You saw Angie? Good for you."

In fact, it was good for him. It was wonderful to see Angie when he stopped by her house unannounced, and it seemed as if she was glad that he had stopped by. Later, however, he wondered if, in Angie's mind, they had gone beyond an estrangement but only to the point of a casual friendship. If so, he might be pressing his luck to try to see her again so soon. Then again, what was there to lose? He might have only a couple of months left in Knittersville anyway.

This time, he called before showing up on her doorstep. He screwed up his courage and called Angie two days after dinner at her house. He was nervous as he dialed her number, more nervous about calling a girl at any time since junior high school. He hoped his voice wouldn't crack as he asked her if she was free for a walk on Sunday.

Sunday was a warm day, a day that promised the imminent arrival of spring. They began their walk by discussing their hopes for an early spring and their concerns that winter was not really over. Their conversation progressed from the weather to more personal concerns; Angie's worries that KnitWare might not get enough business in the next few months, and there could be layoffs, and his hopes that his seminar on Wednesday would go well and give him a shot at the position in Kester's Economics Department. They then walked on for a time in silence.

"David, I've been thinking about our conversation last week, and I want to say that I'm sorry that I said it was just a job. That was insensitive. I know you've worked really hard for this. It must be scary to think that it might not work out."

"That's okay. You were right. I got so wrapped up in all of this that I must've become pretty boring to be around. It's just that the chance to get a tenure-track job finally seemed so close."

"It could still work out," she said encouragingly. "Even if it doesn't, couldn't you keep getting these temporary positions until it eventually does works out?"

"The problem is, I'm not sure something will ever work out. The longer you go without landing a permanent position, the more you look like damaged goods. You can cobble together something from one year to the next, but you can't make a decent living like that."

"Is there something else you could do?"

"I guess, but I like teaching. And I think I'm good at it. Like last fall, there were a few times when I felt I was really getting to the students. I wasn't just teaching them about economics, I was teaching them how to think. These kids are bright, but most of them never really had to think. Sure, they had to memorize stuff, and sometimes they even had to be clever about how to approach a test. But in high school you only take in information and then spit it back out on an exam. Hell, a lot of courses at Kester probably do that, too. But in this class, they were using their brains to ask really good questions. It's a lot harder to ask a good question than to answer one. But there they were, learning pretty sophisticated stuff, asking the right questions, not letting each other get away with easy, facile answers, not even letting themselves get away with easy answers. It was great."

She looked at him for a minute as they walked on. "David, I was wrong. It isn't just a job for you. My jobs haven't been like that. I mean, I liked the challenges, and I liked my coworkers, but, at the end of the day, it was still just a job."

"But that's good, in a way. In grad school I started to define myself, all of me, by how well I did in my studies. And it wasn't just me. All of us were constantly ranking ourselves against each other, and against some idea of where we should be. If you got an A on an exam, then you didn't just think you did well on that exam, you thought it was a sign that you were really smart. It was a short step from thinking that you were smart to thinking that you were going to be successful, and from there to thinking that you were going to be happy. It was a weird, narrow, competitive world that doesn't really leave you very happy after all, even if it all works out."

"Well, what will you do on Wednesday?"

"I have some ideas, but I want to talk to Jeff tomorrow and see what he thinks."

And so, the next day, he knocked on Jeff's door and invited him to lunch. When they sat down with their Caesar salads, Jeff mentioned how many posters he had seen announcing David's seminar, and the fact that, unlike the other job market talks, his was followed by a reception. "That must show that they really like you."

"I don't think that's it. Bill Crocker, the head of CROSS, is coming to the seminar along with a writer for the *Liberty Review*. The school is probably hoping to get some good publicity. The problem is, Crocker has a lot invested in 'Something for Nothing' being correct. He thinks that a magazine article could really help him. I think he's coming all the way to Kester to make sure that I toe the line."

"But what can he do to you if you don't?"

"He said that, as soon as he got back to Virginia, he would call Wellingham and tell him that he just found out that I falsified the data just to get CROSS to publish my work."

"They won't believe that!"

"They might. And even if they aren't totally convinced by Crocker, he could make them wonder about me enough to think it's not worthwhile to take the risk of hiring me."

"David, even if you say the results are right, and Crocker doesn't try to ruin you, eventually people will find out that 'Something for Nothing' was wrong, and that would hurt you down the line."

"I know, but maybe people will just forget about the paper, or maybe Crocker won't have an interest in it after a few years. But the thing is, I would feel like such a fraud if I just out-and-out lied and presented results that I knew were wrong."

Just then, he saw Randolph Carlson holding a tray with his lunch on it and looking around the cafeteria. Randolph caught his eye and, smiling at him, walked over to the table where they were sitting.

"Can I join you?"

"Sure," said David, which, while the only polite response, was not the one that he really wanted to make.

After settling in, Randolph said, "I've seen posters for your seminar all over the place, David. Looks like they've put the seminar in a big room, too, and with a reception following. We in Sociology don't seem to rank like you economists. We don't get that kind of treatment for our talks. Must be an important talk, at least as far as economics goes."

"It's important for me. It's my job market seminar."

"They must really want you here if they're advertising your talk so intensively, and even paying for a reception afterward."

"It's not that. It's because a magazine is covering the talk."

"Do say? What magazine?"

He did not really want to continue with this conversation, and regretted revealing as much as he had, but there was no way to go now but forward. "The *Liberty Review*."

Randolph looked truly outraged, partly because it was a look that he had practiced often. "I knew economics was corrupted by the extreme right, but I never thought I would see someone at my college courting the *Liberty Review*!"

"The *Liberty Review* is more libertarian than it is extreme right," Jeff offered.

"Oh, come on, Jeff. We all know that it's water from the same poisoned well."

"Randolph, the *Liberty Review* actually comes out with some interesting positions," Jeff answered.

"Like their position on homosexual marriage? Speaking of coming out and all."

Jeff and David both stared at Randolph. David was the first one to speak.

"Randolph, what the hell? Jeff's up for tenure this year. You shouldn't go around talking about stuff you don't know about. Some of the older faculty might take it wrong."

"David, you are such an innocent. But I guess that comes with your field, right? I mean, you economists just think of people as machines that buy and sell. Though I suppose there are times when you think of people, or at least students, as more than machines."

"What are you saying?" asked David, as he tried to remember if Jenny Lake was taking a class with Carlson.

"You might ask your friend Jeff about some of his work with a particular student a few years ago. His name was Russell, wasn't it, Jeff?"

David looked at Jeff and felt his heart skip as he saw his friend, his best friend on campus, turn ashen. He felt his anger rise, and it was the anger that spoke when he snarled, "Go fuck yourself, Randolph."

Randolph felt aggrieved. As a senior, tenured professor, it was within his rights to tease these assistant professors; hell, one of them was just a visitor. This little twerp didn't have the right to curse him, though. He avoided his first response, which was to return the curse with one of his own. No, he could get even, and not just mad. He stood and picked up his tray and said, just before walking away, "Well, it will be interesting to see if, in fact, your seminar is more sophisticated than the usual economics claptrap. I'm looking forward to attending it, and I will certainly recommend it to my students as well." With that, he turned and walked off to the other side of the cafeteria.

Jeff and David stared at Randolph as he stalked off. They sat in silence for a minute.

"I'm sorry, Jeff. I shouldn't have lost it like that."

"He had it coming. If he wanted to screw up my tenure case, he'd be doing it regardless of what you said. I don't think he's got it in for me. He just likes to jerk people around. At least I hope he doesn't have it in for me." Jeff paused. "But you, my friend, you now have an enemy. Got any other good strategies for your job talk?"

Chapter 44

Room 1 is the largest and most modern classroom in Central Hall. The stage at the front of the room is raised a step's height above the floor. Standing at the lectern on the stage, a speaker looks out at over one hundred fifty cushioned seats arranged in a gently rising slope from the front of the room to its back. A speaker would not be faulted for thinking he was inside a modern version of a Greek amphitheater or, with a less congenial audience, the Roman Colosseum.

David felt himself more in the Colosseum than in an amphitheater in the minutes before he was to begin his seminar on Wednesday afternoon. As he stood at the lectern, waiting to be introduced by Professor Wellingham, he looked out and saw Bill Crocker and Mason Freeman sitting next to each other in the front of the room. Crocker looked at him intently, occasionally giving him a slight smile and a small nod. As promised, Randolph Carlson was also in attendance. He sat in the back of the room, surrounded by a number of his students. Scattered throughout the rest of the room were members of the Economics Department faculty, the dean of the college, and some of David's students who were either curious about what their teacher did when he wasn't teaching or else willing to sit through another lecture by their professor in order to get some free food afterward. Jenny Lake was there, sitting in the second row and holding hands with Stephen Conley. She caught David's eye and gave him an encouraging smile. In fact, if he had to guess, David would think that the majority of the people in the room did not want to see him fail. There were, however, clearly a few out there who were rooting for the lions rather than the (metaphorical) Christian.

There was little doubt that Randolph and his troops were among those who were not hoping to see him offer a smashing example of the use of economic theory and statistical methods. They sat in the back, like unruly students in a classroom, chatting and joking among themselves as they waited for the seminar to begin. It was less clear what Crocker was hoping for. Crocker might want to see him succeed, if that success was on Crocker's terms. If he wandered too far from Crocker's preferred script, however, it could come down to a question of Crocker or Fox, and, in that case, it was clear what the director of CROSS would want.

Wellingham had brought Crocker and Freeman to David's office about an hour ago. He learned that the three of them, along with the dean of the college, had met for an hour or so immediately after their arrival on the Kester campus, and that their discussion had centered on how Kester could be well represented in the *Liberty Review*. When they arrived at his office, Crocker greeted him warmly, as if they were close colleagues being reunited after a long absence when, in fact, it was the first time they met face-to-face. When Crocker had said to him, "I'm so much looking forward to your seminar. I know you won't disappoint us," David thought he detected a slight rise in his eyebrow that emphasized a meaning of that statement known only to the two of them.

Mason Freeman was much harder to read. He greeted David cordially, but with some reserve. He had told him how he was very interested in his research and had been doing his homework on the topic. When David mentioned that he hoped Freeman didn't find the work too boring, he responded, "Oh no. As a writer I like to learn about a wide range of things, and also about people and organizations. I find it really interesting and often a good challenge." That was all he said about that, but David had the feeling that there was another layer of meaning to his words.

"Good afternoon, good afternoon." Wellingham began, trying to get the audience to quiet down. He continued, "We are very pleased to have our own Professor David Fox speaking to us today about his article "Something for Nothing," a title that seemingly goes against all we hold dear in economics." He paused for the laughter that did, in fact, follow. "As you know, Professor Fox is a visiting professor of economics here at Kester. He is a recent graduate of Columbia University, where he received his doctorate a little less than a year ago. His research has already gained national attention, and we look forward to learning from him today."

David looked down at his handwritten notes one last time during Wellingham's introduction. It was all a lie. But was that such a bad thing? He thought he could navigate a course that would provide him some modicum of intellectual honesty during his passage between the Scylla of Crocker and the Charybdis of Carlson. The real question, however, was whether this talk would also satisfy those sitting in the middle of the room, especially those who would be deciding his future, or lack thereof, at Kester College.

There was a polite smattering of applause following Wellingham's introduction. David walked to the lectern and placed his notes in front of him. He looked across the room. So many lies.

Jeff's life. Jenny's advances. Who knew what Carlson, or Crocker, kept hidden? He imagined the lies as balloons, filling the hall. There was even a big balloon over this building that had, so far, escaped its alternate life as a factory.

"It's a pleasure to be here today." Another lie.

"Thank you for that kind introduction, Professor Wellingham." Well, he was thankful for that nice gesture. Time to focus.

"As you may know, the research in the paper 'Something for Nothing' is about a government program to promote teenage abstinence. This is an important question, since 30 percent of teenage girls get pregnant before the age of twenty. Two-thirds of the families begun by young, unwed mothers are poor, and over half of all mothers on welfare had their first child as a teenager. Clearly, issues of early pregnancy and childbearing are linked to other critical social issues like childhood well-being, income disparity, and poverty. Furthermore, teenage sexuality is associated with other health issues like venereal disease and HIV-AIDS."

"The question for social policy then becomes what represents an effective response to the health and economic issues linked to teenage sexuality. One possible policy is to try to promote teenage abstinence. But there are other policies as well, policies that attempt to educate teenagers about the consequences of their actions. These policies . . ."

"David?" It was Crocker, raising his hand and looking a little concerned. David had been getting into the rhythm of the talk and was a little taken aback by the interruption. One was expected to respond to questions posed during a seminar, of course, but this one came a little early and from an unwelcome source.

"Yes, Dr. Crocker, do you have a question?"

"You mention the health and economic issues linked to teenage abstinence. I'm sure you don't mean to minimize the moral issues as well, and the fact that many religions view out-of-wedlock sexual activity as wrong."

"Actually, Dr. Crocker, I won't have much of anything to say about the morality of teenage sexuality. Economics is not really well positioned to discuss morality, but we can use the tools of economics and statistics to try to understand the consequences of policies."

"That's all well and good, David, but at the same time you don't want to minimize the moral dimension, correct?"

"Well, like I said, what I would like to focus on today is what we can learn from statistical analysis to help formulate effective policies, and then we can leave the moral issue up to the political process."

From the back of the room, in a voice filled with self-righteous certainty, Randolph Carlson joined the conversation. "Are you saying, Professor Fox, that it is correct to leave deeply personal issues that are linked to one's liberty, like those of sexuality, up to a political process? I find that an abhorrent position, as would, I'm sure, some of your colleagues."

He managed to keep his voice calm. "No, Professor Carlson, what I'm saying is that, with the tools of economics and statistics, we can understand what the implications of policies are."

"But we cannot, with these tools, understand if these policies are right." Randy was clearly playing to his audience and, by the looks of it, they were enjoying it.

He had to keep the seminar from deteriorating into a two-way conversation. "It's not an issue of what's right or what's wrong, it's a question of what we can know about the effects of a policy."

"I don't need statistical analysis to know that a policy that impinges on a person's liberty, on her most private choices, is wrong."

He could have just acknowledged Carlson's question and moved on. But he didn't. "Presumably you would want to know the effects of a policy."

"Oh, I know what the effects are," replied Randolph. "The effects are to erode our liberties. And your so-called analysis is just an excuse for the power elite to control people's most private desires." There was a smattering of applause from Carlson's young accolades who, presumably, didn't want the power elite to do anything to lessen their chances to have sex.

"Kids' private desires, Randolph. Surely you would concede that there is a role for the government to limit the sale of alcohol, or cigarettes, to minors?"

"Of course I would, but that is because it is a way to stop capitalist exploitation of children. But government programs to change people's thoughts and views are no more than efforts to suspend liberty."

There was that word again, "liberty," one that Carlson swung around like a mace, and with about the same level of nuance.

It was time to move on. "Well, Randolph, you can decide whether you think the statistical analysis tells us if the government's efforts to control people's actions are effective."

Randolph, however, was not done. Using a well-honed tone of incredulity, he asked, "Do you actually believe statistics?"

"Yes, of course."

"How quaint." Randy's students found this wry comment *très amusant.*

That did it. He felt his voice rise. "What level of arrogance does it take to believe your own intuition, however flawed and however biased by your politics, rather than data that can force a responsible thinking person to reevaluate his own views? The whole point of an education, it seems to me, is to get people to think for themselves, not just to follow what somebody else tells them to think. Sure you might not want to believe that abstinence programs work, but what if they do? We're talking about real people's lives here. Do you want to consign young girls to poverty or disease just because you don't like it if the government promotes responsibility?"

Crocker broke in at this point. "Well said, David. And these abstinence programs do that, don't they? They help people."

He looked at Crocker, and then at his students in the audience, and then at Crocker again. Crocker knew something was up, and he shook his head back and forth while mouthing the word "Don't."

"Let me start my answer to that question with a quote from John Maynard Keynes, one of the greatest economists of the twentieth century. A journalist thought he caught Keynes in what we would now call a flip-flop since he changed his public stance on monetary policy during the Great Depression. Keynes answered the charge by saying to him, 'When the facts change, I change my mind. What do you do, sir?' So a couple of months ago, after my article gained some notoriety, I learned something that made me change my mind about teenage abstinence programs." He allowed himself a look at Crocker, who was clearly fuming. "The best thing that I can teach you today is not so much about abstinence programs, but how you should respect the facts and not let your beliefs about the world be driven by your politics" (directing an obvious look at Randolph at this point) "or your own career" (taking a more surreptitious glance at Crocker). "Instead, you should be driven by a search for truth."

"The truth is often inconvenient. In this case, it was inconvenient for me because I got some attention from my finding about the effectiveness of teenage abstinence programs. It was nice to get that kind of attention, and even helpful. But a friend showed me that I was wrong. I had made a mistake. It was an honest mistake, but it was a mistake just the same. And I'm grateful to that friend. Furthermore, with my friend's help, I was able to correct this mistake and, in that way, learn something new. Today I want to share that new knowledge with all of you."

At this point, the seminar truly began.

Chapter 45

The reception was held in the wide hallway in front of Room 1. Small sandwiches and crudités were lined up on a couple of tables, students dressed in white shirts and black slacks circulated with trays of hot hors d'oeuvres, and a bartender poured wine, beer, and soda. Randolph Carlson and some of his students left before the seminar ended, but the all the others stayed, standing in groups of three or four people, chatting and attempting to balance a glass and a small plate of food.

Murray Stern had come up to David immediately after the seminar and told him that he did a good job. "It's refreshing to hear someone say they initially made a mistake and then learned from it. Usually, we teach as if theories and results were always known. It's good for students to see that we only learn by taking risks and sometimes making mistakes."

"Thanks, Murray." He had thought the seminar went well, but you could never completely tell.

Jeff joined Murray and David at the lectern. "Nice job, David. You did a good job of preparation."

"Thanks for your help, Jeff."

The three of them left the room to join the reception. He glanced around while waiting in line for a glass of wine and spotted Crocker, Freeman, and Wellingham chatting amicably. He wondered how many days Crocker would wait until phoning Wellingham to tell him of his "discovery" of the falsified data.

David also wondered whether this would be his last chance ever to give a seminar. It had been fun. He would miss doing this if things didn't work out. But he also thought that Angie was right: there's more to life than a job. But it's special when you find a job you like. Or would like, if you got it. He was getting tired. He could use a vacation. Maybe Angie could take off a couple of days, and they could go someplace. His thoughts were interrupted by Mason Freeman. "That was a nice talk. It's interesting that your results changed so much, and you ended up finding that abstinence programs weren't effective but sex education was. I was surprised, I didn't think you would have such a complete turnaround from your CROSS working paper."

"Nor did I," said Crocker, who was quick to follow Freeman when he saw that he had gone over to speak with David. "But as we know, David, results are always subject to revision, as more information becomes known." These last comments were directed in a way that left little doubt as to whether Crocker would follow up with his earlier threat.

"Bill, I guess this means that CROSS will have to issue some kind of statement about 'Something for Nothing,'" Freeman said to Crocker.

"Well, Mason, that would be a bit hasty now, wouldn't it. In fact, I was playing around with some corrected data myself just last week, and I think I may be coming up with some interesting results that confirm the original 'Something for Nothing' findings."

"Were you doing this work with Greg Shankle?" Freeman asked.

"No, I was doing it on my own. As you probably know, I've done a fair bit of research on social policies in my younger days."

"Really?" Freeman said, with what appeared to be surprise. "I wasn't able to find any reference to that in my background research on you and on CROSS."

"Well, I don't really talk about it much since it was a while ago, just after I finished my dissertation."

"The funny thing is, Bill, I couldn't find any of your research, or even your dissertation, on publicly available sources. So I called Michigan State, and they didn't have any record of you having completed a PhD there."

Crocker blanched and stared at Freeman without saying anything for what seemed like a long time. David understood that he had just become a witness to, rather than a participant in, a totally new story.

"Mason, these kind of administrative mistakes happen all the time, you must know that. MSU probably just lost my records."

"They did have records about you, Bill, but those indicated that you spent only one year there and left without even a master's degree."

Crocker saw that much more was now at stake than a favorable article in the *Liberty Review*. "After a while, Mason, these degrees are just pieces of paper. After all these years, I think my record speaks for itself."

"That could be, Bill, but there's also an issue about research that was published by the National Tobacco Institute when you worked there. And, of course, we both know about Brockton's paper at CROSS."

Crocker's face had changed from white to red. "What is this article really about, Freeman?"

"Oh you know, Bill, you don't really know where research will lead you when you first start it. I had thought I'd be writing about how places like CROSS were giving an alternative view to the public debate, but now it looks like the article will probably focus on how research is being distorted for political goals."

"I have some powerful friends, Freeman," Crocker said, spitting out the words.

"So do I, Bill," Freeman replied calmly. Turning to David, he continued, "Thanks again for an interesting talk. I learned a lot."

"Me, too," said David.

"Take care," Mason said. "Bill, I can find my own way back to the airport. See you around." With that, he left David and Crocker and exited the reception.

Crocker, his anger now redirected, turned his attention to David.

"You had better not mention this to anyone."

"Bill, you know, I can't imagine not saying something if people get a phone call from you and it becomes my word against yours."

Crocker stared at him for a minute. Finally, he said, "Fine, get a job in some third-rate college. See what I care. But it looks like your friend Greg is going to find it hard to ever graduate from SAVE."

"This has nothing to do with Greg."

"It has everything to do with Greg. And if you aren't going to pay for this, well, he will."

With that, Crocker turned and left. As he was walking out, Professor Wellingham attempted to go over and say good-bye. But Crocker walked past him as if he wasn't even there.

Subject: Berkeley graduate economics
Date: 3/21/2008, 2:05 PM
To: Greg Shankle <Greg.shankle@save.edu>
From: Moses Appelfeld <appelfeld@econ.Berkeley.edu>

Dear Mr. Shankle,

My apologies for not writing back sooner, but I had been traveling and busy with departmental administrative matters.

A few weeks ago I was able to carefully read the letter you sent me with its accompanying short article. I was very impressed. I had thought about doing some work in this area once but set it aside. I'm glad to see that someone else has taken up the challenge.

I agree with your assessment that this may prove to be a popular method to address a range of problems. As to your question about possible errors in your derivation, everything looks correct to me. Of course, when you submit this to a journal it will be subject to closer scrutiny.

Another reason for my delay in writing to you is that, before doing so, I wanted to find out if we had a spot available in our visiting graduate student program. It turns out that I am able to offer you an invitation for next year. The program is well funded, and you would be able to attend classes here. I also have a research assistant position open for next year, and I hope that you would consider that as well. From what I understand from your e-mail, you are already enrolled in a new doctoral program, but perhaps the attractions of the Bay Area could persuade you to apply for full-time status at Berkeley once you've spent some time visiting us.

Please let me know if you would like to follow up with this offer. Even if not, I hope we can stay in contact about this current research and other work you do in the future.

Sincerely,
M. Appelfeld
Moses Appelfeld
Class of 1958 Professor of Economics
Director, Berkeley Econometrics Center

Commencement

Chapter 46

It was going to be a small party, but it promised to be a happy one. Jeff White invited all the members of the Economics Department along with their guests and his other friends to his apartment on the Friday night of commencement weekend to celebrate his official offer of tenure by the Board of Trustees of Kester College earlier that day. The decision had really been made in a series of earlier steps, with the unanimous vote of the Economics Department right after spring break, the vote of the Arts and Sciences Tenure and Promotion Committee a month after that (also unanimous), and the decision of the president of Kester College a week later. And, one could argue, all this had been set in motion even earlier, and over a longer span of time, during those late evenings when Jeff sat alone in his apartment and worked on his research and his class preparation, and when he spent hours patiently explaining economics to students in the classroom and in his office.

The happiness of the guests at the party would come partly from their understanding of the long odds that faced Jeff, or anyone else, in a quest for a tenured position. A small proportion of the bright, ambitious college graduates who apply to doctoral programs are accepted. Many who matriculate leave these programs after only one or two years because of failure, or frustration, or fatigue. Only a subset of those that remain complete the long solitary effort required to successfully write a dissertation. Furthermore, as many can attest, having a PhD provides no guarantee for getting a job. Finally, even those with jobs may fail to get tenure and be forced to move on to another occupation after more than a decade of devoting themselves to their life goal.

Or at least the goal for their professional life. The real challenge, David thought to himself, was not just to get tenure, but to get a life. A tenured position can be a very important component of a life, if one loves the work. But work alone cannot complete a life.

"You've been quiet for a while," Angie said as they walked toward Jeff's apartment. "Is everything okay?"

"Quiet is different from upset. Actually, I was thinking about how glad I am for Jeff, and what a long road it's been for him."

"Are you worried about that road?"

"For me? No, I'm just grateful that I'm going to have a chance to travel down it, at least for a while longer."

He found out that he would have the chance to travel that road during spring break. He and Angie had returned from two days in Montreal early Wednesday afternoon. They stopped at his apartment and found a voice message waiting for him from the chairman of the Economics Department at Sewall College. While Angie sat on the couch, he went to the kitchen to call back. She could tell immediately from the tone of his voice that his dream of landing a tenure-track job had come true. She leapt off the couch and ran into the kitchen and, just barely able to hold off until he hung up the phone, jumped into his arms as soon as he said, "Thanks very much, I'll be back in touch with you soon. Bye."

The rest of that day was spent discussing how they could manage to maintain a relationship if he moved three hundred miles away. There were weekend visits, and, with an academic schedule, many of these could be long weekends. Angie could try to arrange her travel so it took her to the region around Sewall. She also mentioned that there might be new job opportunities for her in central Maine.

But they also knew that there would be challenges. He would work long hours, and his weekends would not be free during the academic year. Angie's job with KnitWare seemed more secure than it had a month earlier, but she, too, was expected to work long hours, including weekends, to help ensure the company's survival. Then there was the question of Giovanna; would Angie be willing to move away from her mother?

Their discussion of how to maintain a relationship, however, avoided an issue that each of them considered but neither of them voiced: whether they would maintain a relationship at all. Things were going well now, but experience had shown them both that staying together was hard, and the difficulty was sure to be compounded by regular separation. And while you can plan for separations, and analyze ways to maximize time together, some things have to be taken on faith.

David had never been very good at taking things on faith. He liked to think, however, that he was getting a little better at it.

Events certainly were helping him along this path. Bad news might come in threes, but maybe good things come in twos. A couple of days after the offer from Sewall, Murray Stern phoned to tell him that the Economics Department was offering him a tenure-track position. Murray mentioned how the faculty had been impressed by his seminar, and how they thought it gave students a good idea of how economics was a living subject, and how its lessons grew and changed as research progressed. He thanked Murray and then, forgetting the most basic lesson economics teaches on bargaining, immediately said yes without even asking about salary. He then called Angie who left work early. They spent the rest of that day, and all of the weekend, together.

After the long winter, the true arrival of spring was especially sweet. David and Angie often met after dinner for a walk around Knittersville, walks that were increasingly taken in daylight as March turned into April, and then into May. The rest of the classes during the spring semester also went well. And, at the end of April, David submitted a revision of a dissertation chapter to the *Journal of Environmental Economics*.

Now that classes were over, and a position was secured, there was time during the summer to revise another chapter. There would also be time to do some more work with Greg, who would soon be decamping for Berkeley. He also planned to spend some time preparing a new course that he would be teaching in the fall. Most important, there was more time to spend with Angie.

But right now, he had to go inside and congratulate his friend.